PEERCOIN

HISTORY OF THE FIRST YEAR

A DECENTRALISED CRYPTOCURRENCY
PART OF THE "ALT-ERNATIVE" BOOK SERIES

Peercoin—History of the First Year

by Christopher P. Thompson

Copyright © 2015 by Christopher P. Thompson

Book Author by Christopher P. Thompson

Book Design by C. Ellis

ISBN-13—978-1512178067
ISBN-10—1512178063

PEERCOIN

HISTORY OF THE FIRST YEAR

A DECENTRALISED CRYPTOCURRENCY
PART OF THE "ALT-ERNATIVE" BOOK SERIES

CHRISTOPHER P. THOMPSON

ABOUT THE AUTHOR

Christopher Paul Thompson is an avid cryptocurrency enthusiast from the United Kingdom. Born in Bradford, UK and academically educated at the University of York (BSc Mathematics). He has been a keen follower of past and current events in the cryptocurrency space since March 2013. His first book called Cryptocurrency "The Alt-ernative" A Beginner's Reference is the first book he has ever written.

Other titles planned for release soon are:

"Reddcoin—History of the First Year"

"DigiByte—History of the First Year"

"Quark—History of the First Year"

"Dash—History of the First Year"

"Dogecoin—History of the First Year"

"Cryptographic Decentralised
Currencies and Assets—
The "Alt-ernative" Book"

E-mail Contact: chris_thompson25@live.co.uk
Twitter Contact: https://twitter.com/MrSilverCider

CONTENTS

CONTENTS

INTRODUCTION

Cryptocurrency was born with the advent of Bitcoin. It was first mentioned in a research paper published online titled "Bitcoin: A Peer-to-Peer Electronic Cash System" with the real name or pseudonym Satoshi Nakamoto attributed to it. This paper was published on the 31st of October 2008. About two months later on the 3rd of January 2009, the Bitcoin network protocol was launched. This technological breakthrough was the beginning of a decentralized public ledger. It allows people to send value across the globe without the permission of a third party authority.

Since then, a growing number of people around the world have been introduced to or discovered cryptocurrency. Many cryptocurrencies have been launched over the proceeding years since the introduction of Bitcoin. The term "alternative" was given to those cryptocurrencies after Bitcoin because they were introduced, implemented and developed to be used instead of or alongside Bitcoin. One could say, a choice of brand in cryptocurrency exists. People have discovered these either through word of mouth, by accident, through personal investigation or via the media. Nevertheless, it has changed the lives of many people. It has provoked the general public into asking innumerable questions about many issues based on subjects such as economics, politics, philosophy, mathematics and so on.

In this book, I hope to give the reader insight into how one particular alternative cryptocurrency began. Peercoin is a relatively old cryptocurrency in the sense that it has been around for nearly three years at the time of publication of this book. This book, as well as other future books to be written on other cryptocurrencies, is a historical story of the first year until the blockchain reached its one year anniversary. It also describes the terminology one encounters such as proof of work mining, block reward, wallets and so on.

INTRODUCTION

I chose to write only about the first year for various reasons, some of which are:

- For almost all cryptocurrencies, the first year of their existence is the most defining period.

- If I had chosen to write a full history of Peercoin, I would be continuously playing catch up.

- Most other cryptocurrencies are not two years old yet, so I have limited the scope of all books on individual cryptocurrencies at this time.

- Currently I have a full-time job besides being a cryptocurrency author, so my time is unfortunately limited.

You may have bought this book because Peercoin is your favourite cryptocurrency. Alternatively, you may be keen to find out how it all began. I have presented the information henceforth without going into too much technical discussion about Peercoin. If you would like to investigate further, I recommended that you read material currently available online at the official website at www.peercoin.net. Also, the official forum at www.peercointalk.org has masses of information via which one can contact some of those people involved in the development of Peercoin.

If you choose to purchase a certain amount of Peercoin, please do not buy more than you can afford to lose.

Enjoy the book :D

WHAT IS PEERCOIN?

Peercoin (originally known as PPCoin) is a cryptocurrency or digital decentralised currency used via the Internet. It is described as a payment network without the need for a central authority such as a bank or other central clearing house. It allows the end user to store or transfer value anywhere in the world with the use of a personal computer, laptop or smartphone (mobile/cellphone). Cryptography has been implemented and coded into the network allowing the user to send currency through a decentralised (no centre point of failure), open source (anyone can review the code), peer-to-peer network. Cryptography also controls the creation of newly mined or minted Peercoin units of account, PPC.

The Peercoin Project began in October 2011. A new form of timestamping called proof of stake was independently discovered by Sunny King and Scott Nadal after studying Nakamoto's work. They had modified a significant proportion of the Bitcoin protocol code. Sunny King pre-announced the launch of the coin nine days in advance on the 10th of August 2012. The general public have been able to use and mine/mint Peercoin since the 19th of August 2012.

The founders and developers of Peercoin describe it as an innovative and unique coin due to the fact it was the first cryptocurrency of its kind. It was the first coin to implement a hybrid timestamping algorithm of proof of work alongside proof of stake. Both these concepts of timestamping are explained later on.

In the appendix of this book, the Peercoin Design White Paper can be found. It goes into the original detail (sometimes technical) of the Peercoin Project.

The slogan used by the Peercoin community to market the coin is:

"THE SECURE & SUSTAINABLE CRYPTOCOIN"

WHY USE PEERCOIN?

Like all cryptocurrencies, people have chosen to adopt Peercoin as a medium of exchange through personal choice. An innovative feature of the coin, an affinity towards the brand or high confidence of the community or developers could be reasons why they have chosen to do so. Key benefits of using Peercoin are:

♦ It is a useful medium of exchange via which value can be transferred anywhere in the world for a fraction of the cost of other conventional methods (e.g. Western Union).

♦ Peercoin eliminates the need for a trusted third party such as a bank, clearing house or other centralised authority (e.g. PayPal). All transactions are solely from one person to another (peer-to-peer).

♦ Peercoin has the potential to engage people worldwide who are without a bank account (unbanked).

♦ Peercoin transactions are irreversible by inherent design.

The official website states a reason why to use Peercoin:

"Peercoin seeks to be the most secure cryptocoin at the lowest cost, by rewarding all users for strengthening the network."

Four official points made by the developers in favour of Peercoin are:

• Built **to Last**—The World's First Proof-of-Stake Coin.

• **Fair** Distribution—No insider pre-sale or instant mining.

• Energy **Efficient**—Mint Peercoins on any device.

• **Transparent** Protocol—The network is fully open source.

IS PEERCOIN MONEY?

Money is a form of acceptable, convenient and valued medium of payment for goods and services within an economy. It allows two parties to exchange goods or services without the need to barter. This eradicates the potential situation where one party of the two may not want what the other has to offer. The main properties of money are:

◆ **As a medium of exchange**—money can be used as a means to buy/sell goods/services without the need to barter.

◆ **A unit of account**—a common measure of value wherever one is in the economic system in which it is accepted.

◆ **Portable**—easily transferred from one party to another. The medium used can be easily carried.

◆ **Durable**—all units of the currency can be lost, but not destroyed.

◆ **Divisible**—each unit can be subdivided into smaller fractions of that unit.

◆ **Fungible**— each unit of account is the same as every other unit within the medium (1 PPC = 1 PPC)

◆ **As a store of value**—it sustains its purchasing power (what it can buy) over long periods of time.

Peercoin easily satisfies the first six characteristics. Taking into account the last characteristic, the value of Peercoin, like all currencies, comes from people willing to accept it as a medium of exchange for payment of goods or services. As it gets adopted by more individuals or merchants, its intrinsic value tends to increase accordingly.

PEERCOIN SPECIFICATION

Here are sixteen characteristics of the Peercoin network protocol. As can be seen, the coin was announced nine days in advance of launch without any pre-mine:

Coin Symbol:	Ᵽ
Unit of account:	PPC
Date of Announcement:	10th of August 2012 14:18:31 UTC
Genesis Block Generated:	16th of August 2012 02:31:27 UTC
Date of Launch:	19th of August 2012 18:19:16 UTC
Founders:	Sunny King/Scott Nadal
Hashing Algorithm:	SHA-256
Timestamping Algorithm:	Hybrid proof of work/proof of stake
Address Begins With:	P
Total Coins:	No limit (3-5% inflation in early 2015)
Proof of Stake Block Time:	~10 minutes
Proof of Work Block Time:	0.5—2 hours (Initially ~10 minutes)
Difficulty Retarget Time:	~10 minutes (every block)
Coins per Block:	Initially 2,499.75 PPC
Confirmations per Transaction:	6
Pre-mine*:	None

*A pre-mine generally refers to the number of coins mined/minted by the founder or developers before it is officially launched to the public.

PEERCOIN MILESTONE TIMELINE

10th of August 2012	—Peercoin pre-announced on the Bitcointalk forum.
16th of August 2012	—Peercoin genesis block generated.
16th of August 2012	—Peercoin blockchain date of launch announced.
19th of August 2012	—Peercoin Design White Paper and release build clients publicly made available.
19th of August 2012	—Peercoin blockchain launched.
19th of August 2012	—New official Peercoin Bitcointalk thread created.
26th of August 2012	—www.ppcointalk.org forum created by FuzzyBear.
26th of August 2012	—PPCoin subreddit created (.../r/ppcoin)
26th of August 2012	—Sunny King's first weekly update published.
1st of September 2012	—Version 0.2.0 of the Peercoin protocol released.
4th of September 2012	—Cryptocoin became the first exchange to trade PPC.
7th of September 2012	—Bitparking became the second exchange to trade PPC.
10th of September 2012	—Peercoin blockchain switched to v0.2.0 protocol.
18th of September 2012	—Generation of the first proof of stake block.
18th of September 2012	—First Peercoin block explorer created.
2nd of October 2012	—Sunny King weekly updates began to be published on a separate Bitcointalk thread.
3rd of October 2012	—Number of PPC generated surpassed ten million.
15th of October 2012	—Block number 10,000 reached.
16th of November 2012	—Vircurex became the third exchange to trade PPC.
19th of November 2012	—Version 0.2.2 of the Peercoin protocol released.
28th of November 2012	—Bitcoin block reward halved at block number 210,000.

PEERCOIN MILESTONE TIMELINE

3rd of December 2012	—First payment processor of Peercoin created.
10th of December 2012	—All time high of proof of work mining difficulty in 2012 of 43,120 reached at block number 19,080.
15th of December 2012	—Block number 20,000 reached.
26th of December 2012	—Number of PPC generated surpassed fifteen million.

Year 2013

28th of January 2013	—Completion of the v0.3.0 protocol code.
9th of February 2013	—First fork of Peercoin launched called Novacoin.
18th of February 2013	—Version 0.3.0 of the Peercoin protocol released.
19th of March 2013	—Peercointalk.org forum established by FuzzyBear.
20th of March 2013	—Peercoin blockchain switched to v0.3.0 protocol.
5th of April 2013	—Bitparking exchange closed.
6th of April 2013	—BTC-e exchange began to trade PPC.
9th of April 2013	—Peercoin market capitalisation reached a new all time high of about $8.08 million. One PPC was ~$0.44.
22nd of April 2013	—Sunny King's first post on peercointalk.org made.
24th of April 2013	—Bter exchange began to trade PPC.
29th of April 2013	—Directvoltage.com was the first retailer to accept PPC as payment form. Holy Angels Church in Chicago, USA was the first charitable organization to accept PPC.

PEERCOIN MILESTONE TIMELINE

1st of May 2013	—Community began to design and post new Peercoin coin logos.
2nd of May 2013	—New subreddit created (.../r/peercoin).
2nd of May 2013	—Second fork of Peercoin launched called Bitbar.
8th of May 2013	—Third fork of Peercoin launched called Yacoin.
16th of May 2013	—Fourth fork of Peercoin launched called Bitgem.
22nd of May 2013	—Peercoin tipping went live on reddit.
23rd of May 2013	—Cryptsy exchange began to trade PPC.
26th of May 2013	—Crypto Trade exchange began to trade PPC.
7th of June 2013	—99Designs fund raising began.
13th of June 2013	—Funding goal reduced from $800 to $300.
18th of June 2013	—Funding goal reached for the 99Designs logo contest.
22nd of June 2013	—Coins-e exchange began to trade PPC.
28th of June 2013	—Primecoin pre-announced on Bitcointalk.
1st of July 2013	—Silver package on 99Designs ($499) chosen.
7th of July 2013	—Sunny King launched his second cryptocurrency called Primecoin, XPM.
13th of July 2013	—Brand new Peercoin coin logo chosen.
28th of July 2013	—Crypto Trade added the pairs XPM/PPC and XPM/USD.
4th of August 2013	—Chat Box added to the main page of the official Peercoin forum.
8th of August 2013	—Vitalik of Bitcoin Magazine interviewed Sunny King.
19th of August 2013	—Peercoin blockchain celebrated first anniversary.

WHAT IS PROOF OF WORK/STAKE?

Proof of work and proof of stake are both referred to collectively as timestamping methods. They are the methods used to secure the Peercoin network in order to sustain decentralisation and validate transactions. Therefore, no third party needs to be trusted to verify and then add transactions the blockchain.

Proof of work mining is currently used in the decentralised network protocol of Bitcoin thanks to the research by Satoshi Nakamoto. Miners commit the processing (hashing) power of their computers towards successfully finding blocks either individually or as part of a group with other miners (mining pool). As the cumulative hash of the network increases, the network becomes more secure.

Proof of stake was independently discovered by Sunny King after he studied the work of Nakamoto. It was introduced into Peercoin alongside proof of work on the 19th of August 2012. Users of the wallet client help to secure the network by keeping their clients active. When coins arrive in a given wallet address, they begin to age. If the user chooses to hold a certain number of coins in this address for a minimum of thirty days, they then become eligible (have a certain probability) to receive new coins or a stake based on an overall 1% annual rate of interest.

Since the 18th of September 2012, the ratio of the number of blocks generated via proof of stake to those mined by proof of work has grown. In 2015, there are now about five times as many proof of stake blocks than proof of work blocks generated.

Proof of stake is widely accepted as the environmentally friendly way to timestamp transactions to the blockchain instead of the high energy cost of proof of work.

Many other coins have implemented proof of stake into their network protocols since its introduction. Novacoin was the first cryptocurrency to adopt proof of stake into their network protocol on the 9th of February 2013.

PROOF OF WORK MINING

Proof of work mining is a competitive computerised process which helps to maintain and secure the blockchain in such a way as to verify transactions and prevent double spending. It was used in Peercoin as a means to build up the initial coin circulation and still is used today to sustain a certain inflation.

In the general sense of cryptocurrency, those who participate in the activity of mining are called miners. They are general members of the cryptocurrency community who dedicate processing power (hash) of their computers towards solving highly complex mathematical problems and verifying transactions. This process upholds the integrity and security of the network. As such, miners are described as protectors of the network. Each transaction (held within a certain block) is validated before adding it to the blockchain. By doing this, they are rewarded (as an incentive) with newly generated mined coins or transaction fees. These coins are issued by the software in a transparent and predictable way outside of the control of its founders and developers. A miner can be based anywhere in the world as long as they have an internet connection, sufficient knowledge of how one mines and the hardware/software required to do so.

Miners use GPUs (Graphical Processing Units) or CPUs (Central Processing Units) to process transactions by hashing. Also, Application Specific Integrated Circuits (ASICs) allow miners to use customised hardware for faster and lower power mining.

Peercoin also uses proof of stake timestamping that has become more prominent over time. It is the objective of the Peercoin founder, Sunny King, and the developers of the coin to achieve a fully proof of stake, environmentally friendly cryptocurrency in the near future.

PEERCOIN BLOCKCHAIN

Every cryptocurrency has a corresponding blockchain within its decentralised network protocol. Peercoin is no different in this sense. A blockchain is simply described as a general public ledger of all transactions and blocks ever executed since the very first block. In addition, it continuously updates in real time each time a new block is successfully mined or minted. Blocks enter the blockchain in such a manner that each block contains the hash of the previous one. It is therefore utterly resistant to modification along the chain since each block is related to the prior one. Consequently, the problem of doubling-spending is solved.

As a means for the general public to view the blockchain, web developers have created block explorers. The first block explorer for Peercoin was created on the 18th of September 2012 by user "dreamwatcher". It was made available online via the URL link http://www.ppcexplore.org:2750/. An amended link was created at www.ppcexplore.org later on, but this page no longer exists.

Since the inception of the first block explorer, other websites have been created. Currently available explorers include the following:

- https://bkchain.org/ppc;

- https://blockexplorer.peercointalk.org/

- https://bitinfocharts.com/ppcoin/explorer/;

- http://ppc.blockr.io/;

- https://coinplorer.com/PPC

- http://explorer.coinpayments.net/index.php?chain=12

PEERCOIN BLOCKCHAIN

By visiting and browsing these explorer sites, only the second one is specifically for Peercoin. It is the official block explorer of Peercoin. One can easily access the site by visiting the official Peercointalk forum, selecting the "Community" tab, clicking on the "Peercointalk Services" option and then selecting the Peercoin Block Explorer. At the bottom of this explorer site, it clearly states; "Brought to you by FuzzyBear and PeercoinTalk.org".

Block explorers tend to present different layouts, statistics and charts. Some are more extensive in terms of the information given. Some statistics include:

- **Height of the block—** the block number of the network.

- **Time of the block—** the time at which the block was stamped to the blockchain.

- **Transactions—** the number of transactions in that particular block.

- **Total Sent—** the total amount of cryptocurrency sent in that particular block.

- **Reward of the block—** how many coins were generated in the block (added to overall coin circulation).

It is also possible to find out the type of block generated. That is, whether a certain generated block was either proof of work or proof of stake. The opening page of https://blockexplorer.peercointalk.org/ shows the current state of the Peercoin network protocol. An example of the statistics shown is on the adjacent page. It was the screenshot on the 4th of May 2015 at about 16:20 UTC.

PEERCOIN BLOCKCHAIN

Network Hashrate:	293.49 TH/s
Total Coins:	22,281,765
Price:	0.222217 USD / 0.000933532 BTC
Market Capitalization:	4951386.03735 USD
PoS Difficulty:	16.11125889
PoW Difficulty:	171015935.45032
PoS Minting Reward (last 1h/24h):	94.98 / 891.72
Average PoS Minting Reward (last 1h/24h):	15.83 / 8.18
PoW Mining Reward (last 1h/24h):	0 / 3095.87
Average PoW Mining Reward (last 1h/24h):	0 / 88.45
Total Blocks:	172,419
PoS Blocks (last 1h/24h):	6 / 109
PoW Blocks (last 1h/24h):	0 / 35
PoS:PoW Ratio 1h/24:	1:0 / 109:35

PPC PROOF OF WORK BLOCK REWARD

On the 19th of August 2012 at about 18:20 UTC, the first block was found via proof of work mining. This block generated a total of 2,499.75 new PPC units of account ready to participate in the Peercoin economy. Only proof of work blocks were mined until the first proof of stake block on the 18th of September 2012, about thirty days after launch. The following table shows the first ten blocks found:

Block Number	Time of Block	PPC generated
1	2012-08-19 18:19:16 UTC	2,499.75
2	2012-08-19 18:19:28 UTC	2,499.75
3	2012-08-19 18:25:24 UTC	2,498.53
4	2012-08-19 18:27:31 UTC	2,498.03
5	2012-08-19 18:28:02 UTC	2,497.03
6	2012-08-19 18:30:09 UTC	2,495.86
7	2012-08-19 18:38:58 UTC	2,494.88
8	2012-08-19 18:41:10 UTC	2,494.73
9	2012-08-19 18:53:12 UTC	2,493.75
10	2012-08-19 18:55:46 UTC	2,493.01

As can be seen from the first ten blocks, it is clear that the spacing between blocks is not the stated 10 minutes. Blocks were initially found at a faster rate due to high hashing power committed to the network alongside the slow adjustment process in the difficulty to successfully find these blocks. At the time of publication, there are approximately five times as many blocks found via proof of stake than proof of work. Also, proof of stake blocks generate very few PPC in contrast to a proof of work block.

PPC PROOF OF WORK BLOCK REWARD

$$\left\{ \frac{9,999^{4}}{\text{DIFFICULTY}} \right\}^{1/4}$$

Unlike the vast majority of cryptocurrencies, including Bitcoin, Peercoin does not have a pre-determined schedule of how many PPC are generated per block between two dates. There are no block halving dates to look forward to, but there is a formula implemented into the protocol code that determines reward per block. As can be seen above, the block reward of each proof of work block is dependent on the difficulty figure for that particular block. This, in turn, is dependent on the overall computational hashing power committed to finding these blocks. One can easily calculate the block reward of the first block by using the initial difficulty figure of 256. That is, 2,499.75 PPC.

BLOCK TIME OF PEERCOIN

The block time is the average time taken for the network to successfully generate a certain block either by proof of work or proof of stake. Both the reward and time of all blocks generated dictate how the circulation of coins grows over time.

Initially, the proof of work block time of Peercoin was an average of ten minutes. At this time, the block reward was above 2,000 PPC. This meant the circulation of coins grew quickly in its initial distribution phase. Currently, the block time of a proof of work block is between forty and fifty minutes with an associated block reward of just below ninety PPC. Consequently, the number of PPC added to the overall circulation from proof of work mining has fallen significantly over time.

Since the 18th of September 2012, the Peercoin protocol has been generating proof of stake blocks. Peercoin proof of stake block times have continued to tend towards a fixed target of ten minutes. They have become more frequent and generate a much smaller number of PPC than proof of work blocks. As a result, the inflation of the total number of Peercoin in circulation has decreased to levels of 3-4%. Peercoin's annual inflation rate averaged at below 5% during the year 2014.

The following chart displays the growth of the PPC money supply for the first year of Peercoin. On the 16th of August 2013, the total supply surpassed 20 million.

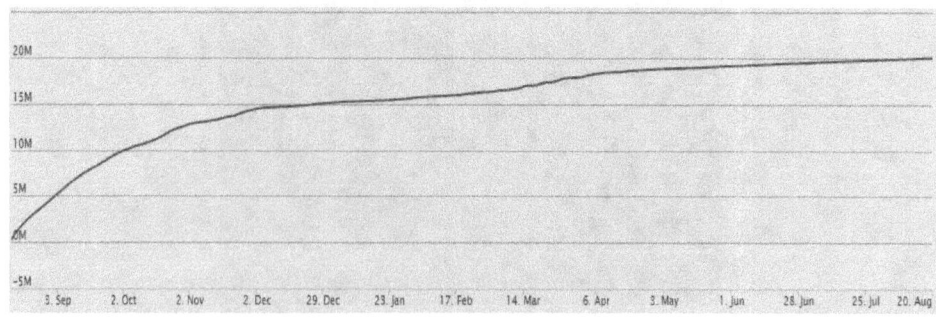

PEERCOIN WALLETS

A wallet is basically a piece of software that can be used on a personal computer, tablet or smartphone. It allows users to store Peercoins as well as execute transfers of PPC with other users. Alternatively, it can be described as a means to access the coins from the inseparable blockchain (public transaction ledger). The wallet cryptographically generates and holds the public and private keys necessary to make these transactions possible. The software can be accessed, downloaded and installed from the official page:

- http://www.peercoin.net/wallet

Peercoin wallets have been developed to work on the operating systems Windows, Mac OS X and Linux. Peercoin has two desktop wallets called Peerunity and Peercoin-QT. By visiting the above official wallet page, the Peerunity wallet is recommended for most users. Peerunity has been developed by the Peercoin community and includes features beyond the core protocol QT wallet. As shown below, there are five different types of wallet available to the general public:

PEERUNITY   **PEERCOIN-QT**   **PAPER WALLET**

ANDROID WALLET   **BKCHAIN WALLET**

FIRST YEAR PEERCOIN EXCHANGES

During the first year of Peercoin, a total of eight known cryptocurrency exchanges introduced Peercoin to their trading platform. At this moment in time (May 2015), Peercoin has ceased to trade on some of these exchanges.

Dates on which Peercoin was added to the below exchanges have been discovered by reading announcements on official forum threads or by using the website called www.cryptocoincharts.info, a site that conveniently charts the BTC price of one unit of PPC.

The last recorded trade on Crypto Trade was on the 28th of January 2015.

First day trading volume on Bitparking was over 200,000 PPC. This exchange closed on the 5th of April 2013, one day before trading on BTC-e began.

Name of Exchange	Trading Against	Status	Date Added
CryptoCoin		CLOSED	~4th of September 2012
BitParking		CLOSED	~7th of September 2012
Vircurex	BTC	ACTIVE	~16th of November 2012
BTC-e	BTC and USD	ACTIVE	~6th of April 2013
Bter	BTC, LTC and CNY	ACTIVE	~24th of April 2013
Cryptsy	BTC, LTC, XRP and USD	ACTIVE	~23rd of May 2013
Crypto Trade		CLOSED	~28th of May 2013
Coins-e	BTC	ACTIVE	~22nd of June 2013

CURRENT PEERCOIN EXCHANGES

As of the 12th of April 2015, there are a total of 31 exchanges or methods to buy Peercoin directly. A cryptocurrency exchange is a site on which registered users can buy or sell Peercoin against BTC, LTC, USD and so on. Some exchanges require users to fully register by submitting certain documentation including proof of identity and address. On the other hand, a lot of exchanges only require users to register with a simple username and password with the use of a currently held e-mail account. The following is a table of currently active exchanges:

Exchange	Location	Exchange	Location
247exchange	Belize	Cryptonit	England & Wales
AllCoin	British Virgin Islands	Cryptsy	United States
Anycoin Direct	The Netherlands	ExchangeMyCoins	Denmark
Banx.io	Panama	HolyTransactions	United States
Bitspark	Hong Kong	Jubi	China
Bittylicious	England	LiteBit	The Netherlands
Bleutrade	Brazil	Melotic	Hong Kong
BTC38	China	NIX-E	Russia
BTC-e	Bulgaria	Poloniex	United States
BX Thailand	Thailand	PS Coin	United States
CCEDK	Denmark	ShapeShift	—-
Coinbroker	—-	The Rock	Malta
Coinnector	Belize	Tuminium	Mexico
Coinomat	British Virgin Islands	Vircurex	China
Coins-e	Canada	YoBit	—-
Comkort	Estonia		

VIEW OF SUNNY KING

"I worked pretty hard through late 2011 and early 2012 on peercoin, and was thrilled to see the project materialize in front of our eyes. Released August 2012 to public, peercoin became the first to offer an energy efficient alternative design to bitcoin's, and the first to introduce the concept of proof-of-stake with a real design. I was also deeply moved by the community supporting the project. To know many of you sharing similar ideals and contributing lots of effort in the cryptocurrency movement, makes this journey very fulfilling for me."

VIEW OF FUZZYBEAR

"I got into bitcoin in April 2012 through mining on a GPU rig, one 7970 AMD served me well and I learnt a lot about the fundamentals through the mining experience. By this point Bitcoin was worth about $7 a coin and I saw my investment as the GPU and the bitcoins as a side bonus that might be worth something one day. The mining was all done on GPU, and it was dominated by pools, a few large GPU rigs were solomining but slush was the big one, but bitparkings pool was one that stood out as an interest with merged mining altcoins of namecoin, Ixcoin, I0coin and devcoin alongside bitcoin.

LTC was mining with a CPU and I could see the lay of the land for a mass POW mining arms race should the price of bitcoin ever shoot to the moon this would fund the development for LTC GPU miners. The market was happy and filled with people speculating on bitcoin with GPU rigs and anyone unable to afford the GPU was mining LTC with a CPU. Any "clonecoins" back in those days were quickly snuffed out by community members if they showed premining, no announcement, no variation etc.. BBQcoin was one of these as an example.

Then one day while browsing the altcoin section of bitcointalk I see this announcement from SunnyKing that there will be a new coin launched in 9 days and source code released to all at same time in order to try this new POS hybrid method of securing the blockchain. Firstly I liked the style of the post, SunnyKing was announcing the launch date giving everyone time to review the paper and get ready for the launch of the coin so as to give equal opportunity to all in the early stages. Secondly there were a number of familiar big names in the bitcoin world posting, reviewing and commenting on this POS hybrid and how it was going to work. SunnyKing was relentless in answering them all and came across confident in his choices and fundamentals of ppcoin, it was in these early days I became aware that Sunny King was not your average bitcoin user and rather someone whom is very visionary and capable of writing very good code. He inspired me to further myself and strive to know and be able to do more.

VIEW OF FUZZYBEAR

PPCoin was launched and it took me a few days to get completely up and running mining on my GPU, but oh the days when my 7970 with 600MH could mine about 3 blocks in a day and the reward per block was about 1200 PPC. I set 50,000PPC as a target to mine and hold in a wallet to try the POS minting in 30 days. The race was also on to set up a pool for POW mining as there were days I got unlucky and found no blocks. NothinG setup the first pool and most of my coins were mined through there, but I wanted to try and give something extra to the few of us who were interested in this new coin. So I setup https://www.peercointalk.org with a number of guides on how to mine, what your config file should look like etc and ran it as a Drupal forum site. Never run drupal before but inspired by this SunnyKing to try new things and step outside the box. Pretty much immediately swamped by spam on the forum and had to switch eventually to SMF as we are today with its better spam prevention and options.

I had found a new passion in life... Peercoin, with this variation on the bitcoin code suddenly all the github repo's for bitcoin related tools were potential useful coding projects to teach myself new and exciting code. Peercoin was repeatedly said by Sunny to be an experiment and to think about what you are investing, his level-headedness and weekly updates provided the confirmation PPCoin was here to stay and the POW sha-256 worked as an excellent distribution method as a few other pools added PPC (coinotron, bitparking) people became interested in minting blocks especially as the trick was to leave the coins in a wallet for more than 30 days without moving. 95% of all you could do at this point with any bitcoins was gamble it on sites and people would sometimes double up what they mined and most lost all they had mined, so forgetting about coins for a month seemed like a great investment as well.

VIEW OF FUZZYBEAR

The POS environmentally friendly aspect of PPC was not really touted so much in the first year, as POS was yet to be securing the network, but as bitcoin mining went to FPGA and then ASIC the arms race had really begun and suddenly all SHA-256 coins were under threat from 51% attacks if someone ordered all the ASIC's or if an attacker developer the chip first. Suddenly I realised the true brilliance of Sunnyking as PPC was becoming secured by POS at this point and the threat was completely countered by the actual design of the coin. Maintaining a public ledger through POS as the ones that hold the most have the most to loose reduced the heavy expense of maintaining the blockchian through POW. Bitcoin price has always been tied to the cost of electricity and the difficulty of the network, Peercoin allowed for the same public ledger but without the overheads of daily electricity consumption.

Peercoin as a backbone currency is something that SunnyKing has always said, but it was Jordan Lee who made that a reality through the creation of Peershares. I believe there will be some exciting times ahead for Peercoin as more Peershares implementations are launched. The peercoin community has always been there for me, I have had some tough times but there are some great people capable of amazing things when they put their minds to it. Peercoin has attracted some very capable developers and there are some amazing projects like peerbox that just add to the interest peercoin has to offer.

One of the most memorable events for me in Peercoin would be the introduction of ASIC's to the mining scene. Suddenly Peercoin was unique. Never would we see a SHA-256 coin launched with Peercoin's parameters as the security could no longer be guaranteed through POW as a bitcoin pool would easily be able to attack the coin. Peercoin had made another unique feature about it that just made me believe I should invest my time with this coin and community.

Fuzzybear"

VIEW OF SENTINELRV

"I got interested in cryptocurrency around the time of the early 2013 price bubble. Rather than invest in Bitcoin though, I was looking for the next Bitcoin, something which improved on the initial design and I found that in Peercoin. I felt Peercoin was way ahead of its time, given the fact that most people were only focused on proof-of-work based cryptos. The idea of a long-term sustainable and energy efficient cryptocurrency that allowed anyone to fairly participate in the minting process was revolutionary to me. I felt as if I had stumbled upon the future of crypto and nobody else had realized it existed yet.

I immediately got involved and helped push for the rebranding of ppcoin to Peercoin. My most memorable event of the first year was when I managed the 99designs contest to find a new logo for Peercoin. I was brand new to the community at the time and nobody knew who I was. Without any previous reputation in the crypto community, I attempted to raise funds from the community to hold this design contest. While the fundraising was successful, I ended up contributing some extra funds of my own to help advertise the contest to more designers so we would get more submissions. Being in a role such as this is hard because you're essentially balancing what you, the community and Sunny King wanted to see while trying to convey it all to the designers. Luckily, through this process we found the right designer in Lightning and chose his excellent work as the official Peercoin logo. Lightning has gone on to help our community design logos for Primecoin, Peershares, Peerunity and Peerbox.

Looking toward the future, I believe we're going to have some stiff competition. Peercoin is no longer the only crypto based on proof-of-stake and many of our competitors are developing exciting new features.

VIEW OF SENTINELRV

I still feel Peercoin has an edge on them though, due to our nearly 3 year constant distribution of coins via proof-of-work, plus the fact that we still have Sunny King as our caretaker. It took a brilliant mind to develop proof-of-stake consensus and I feel secure in knowing that this same person continues to develop and look out for the best interests of Peercoin. Sunny's careful, security minded approach to development and focus on modular design has gained him a massive amount of trust and respect throughout the crypto community and that trust is not easily replaced by special features developed by competing crypto communities.

I also feel that Bitcoin and proof-of-work will continue to remain dominant for the foreseeable future. Proof-of-stake consensus is still discounted by a large number of people in the crypto community, but it continues to influence more and more people every single day. I believe that Peershares could be the key to legitimizing proof-of-stake as a valid consensus mechanism. Currencies that are based on proof-of-stake like Peercoin will continue to find difficulty in convincing people that they are the solution to the problems of proof-of-work. However, distributed autonomous organizations and corporations (DAOs & DACs) based on Peercoin technology like Peershares will start to grow in numbers. Unlike a cryptocurrency like Peercoin, DAOs and DACs will be able to create consistent profits in the form of crypto dividends for those who own shares in them. I see an entire economy springing up that is formed out of different types of Peershares implementations. The more this economy grows, the more its foundational consensus mechanism (proof-of-stake) will be legitimized, and in my opinion, that can only be good for Peercoin's future."

PEERCOIN COMMUNITY

A community is a social unit or network that shares common values and goals. It derives from the Old French word "comuntee". This, in turn, originates from "communitas" in Latin (communis; things held in common). Peercoin has a community consisting of an innumerable number of individuals who have the coin's well being and future goal at heart. These individuals almost always prefer fictitious names with optional corresponding "avatars". Most notable individuals in the community are Sunny King, Sentinelrv, FuzzyBear, Chronos and Jordan Lee.

At the time of publication, there are social media sites on which much discussion and development of Peercoin occurs. These are:

- **Facebook** - https://www.facebook.com/Peercoin

- **Google +** - https://plus.google.com/+PeercoinNet/posts

- **Official Forum** - https://www.peercointalk.org/

- **Reddit** - https://www.reddit.com/r/peercoin

- **Twitter** - https://twitter.com/PeercoinPPC

- **YouTube** - https://www.youtube.com/user/peercoin

A new official Peercoin Bitcointalk thread was created by Sentinelrv on the 23rd of September 2014, but this thread has not been very active:

- **Bitcointalk thread** - https://bitcointalk.org/index.php?topic=793142.0

In essence, the community surrounding and participating in the development of Peercoin is the backbone of the coin. Without a following, the prospects of future adoption and utilisation are starkly limited. Peercoin belongs to all those who use it, not just to the founder who initially created it.

FIRST YEAR HISTORY OF PEERCOIN

LIST OF CHAPTERS

THE LAUNCH OF PEERCOIN

AUGUST 2012

I.   Sunny King created a pre-release thread on Bitcointalk.

II.   Sunny King created a thread on Bitcointalk to coincide with the launch.

III.   Peercoin Design Paper released.

IV.   FuzzyBear launched Peercoin's very own dedicated chat forum.

V.   Sunny King published his first weekly update.

On the 10th of August 2012 at 14:18:31 UTC, a pre-release forum thread on Bitcointalk was created by Sunny King. It was titled "[ANN] [PPC] PPCoin Beta Release Soon" in anticipation of a future blockchain launch on the 19th of August 2012. He announced Peercoin as the first implementation of a hybrid proof of work and proof of stake cryptocurrency. He was quoted as saying,

> "I am happy to announce that project ppcoin is now close to beta quality and will be released to public soon."

As mentioned previously in the introduction, the Peercoin project began about ten months prior to this announcement. Nevertheless, the cryptocurrency community had now been notified of a new innovative cryptocurrency based on proof of stake together with proof of work as timestamping.

The first Bitcointalk forum user to reply to the initial pre-release Peercoin thread was "HauntingShade" on the 11th of August at 02:49:19 UTC. He was quoted as saying:

> "Sounds good.
> Create a simple but effective Windows (GUI) miner and I'll help during the launch!"

After nine replies on the thread over about four days, Sunny King posted a reply on the 16th of August at 17:50:31 UTC in which he said:

> "We are busy preparing the final build of the release. Official block chain is tentatively scheduled to start at SUNDAY 2012-08-19 18:00:00 UTC
>
> Disclaimer: This is experimental beta software so play at your own risk. We reserve the right to restart block chain should severe flaws require such actions but we will try our best to avoid such scenario as much as possible.
>
> Release builds will be available for download a few hours before the scheduled block chain start time. Source code and design paper will be available around the same time or earlier.
>
> Thank you for your support!"

At that moment, it was clear that a pre-determined launch date had been chosen. This made it possible for those already aware of Peercoin to get ready and also made it possible for others to discover it in the space of about three days.

On the 17th of August at 10:41:2 UTC, user FuzzyBear posted his first comment on the official Bitcointalk Peercoin thread :

> "I will be there on sunday to support you with your coin 😐 best of luck and hope the release goes ahead!!
> Will u be releasing a wallet and miner??"

On the 19th of August at 04:21:04 UTC, Sunny King posted an update to announce the official Peercoin Design White Paper had just been released on the official website at www.ppcoin.org. This was the original Peercoin website designed and created by Sunny King. As can be seen below, the interface comprised of a Grand Theft Auto background and just five different icons, one being the very first recognisable Peercoin coin logo (far left icon). From the left, the clickable icons were links to the design paper, sourcecode, client download, wiki and chat forum.

2012 PPCoin Developers

https://web.archive.org/web/20120821201902/http://www.ppcoin.org/

Also on the 19th, it was announced that the release builds had been completed. Both this and the sourcecode (publicly released on github) were then scheduled to be released about five minutes before the launch time. Shortly after that announcement, a new Bitcointalk forum thread titled "[ANN] [PPC] PPCoin Released! - First Long-Term Energy-Efficient Crypto-Currency" was created at 19:54:28 UTC, again by Sunny King, after the launch. His opening comment was the following:

> "Thank you for your support in our prerelease thread
> https://bitcointalk.org/index.php?topic=99735.0."

Just before the creation of the new official Peercoin Bitcointalk thread, the first block was successfully found at 18:19:16 UTC. This block was generated via proof of work, so the successful miner was rewarded with a total of 2,499.75 PPC. An attributed difficulty of 256 existed at block number one. As can be seen below, a block explorer clearly shows this timestamped block. Block number two was also generated via proof of work, found 12 seconds after the first with the same block reward of 2,499.75.

On the 20th of August, there was a debate over the trust and suitability of centralised checkpointing being acceptable for the coin. The blockchain began with a checkpoint at each proof of work block. This method was viewed as temporary until the network had matured and become more secure.

Peercoin Block Explorer

Block Height: 1	Block Time: 2012-08-19 18:19:16 UTC

Block Version	Block Size	Mint Value
proof-of-work	267	2499.75

Block Bits	Block Nonce	Block Difficulty
1c00ffff	1915373966	256

Merkle Root	1bdae84eff34e15399335fc2a48c70fa6b0b9caf972e38b0e3bda106d223f668
Block Hash	00000000000be4e024af5071ba515c7510767f42ec9e40c5fba56775ff296658

<- Previous Block   Block Time: 2012-08-19 18:19:16 UTC   Next Block ->

1bdae84eff34e15399335fc2a48c70fa6b0b9caf972e38b0e3bda106d223f668

http://blockexplorer.peercointalk.org/index.php?
input=00000000000be4e024af5071ba515c7510767f42ec9e40c5fba56775ff296658

On the 20th of August at 23:27:57 UTC, user "coblee", the founder of Litecoin, left a comment on the Peercoin Bitcointalk thread. He said:

"I'm interested to find out more about this coin. Looking at the code, it seems like Sunny has indeed been working on this since November of last year. So it's unfortunate that he decided to do kind of a rush launch of the coin. The information about how a coin works should really be announced and analyzed by the community before the blockchain is started. Now miners have to decide whether they want to jump in without knowing what they are really supporting or wait until more information is released. Couple this with the fact that the block generation starts at 9999 and decreases as difficulty increases, this coin might turn out to have a larger effective premine than SolidCoin."

The above comment was constructive criticism, but it was not taken personally by the community. On the 24th of August, user "FlipPro" was quoted as saying:

"Have you considered changing the name of this coin? I think it should go up for a vote, because PPC is honestly a terrible name."

Sunny King responded by saying:

"Name is fixed and can no longer be changed. Let's leave it at that. It was meant to mean peer-to-peer, see the coin symbol, two P's connected."

The suggestion by "FlipPro" to alter the name of the coin would not be the last.

In the last week of August, FuzzyBear announced that he was in the process of creating a chat forum specifically for Peercoin. On the 26th of August at 00:26:54 UTC, he notified the community of the new forum (www.ppcointalk.org) on which a better discussion about the coin could occur. He also politely requested users to leave feedback on its design, functionality and ease of navigation. Sunny King responded to the creation of the forum by saying:

> "I am really touched by the enthusiasm and dedication by the small community we have now. I will try to do my best" ☺

Also on the 26th of August, Sunny King published his first weekly update (#1) on the official Peercoin thread of Bitcointalk. He said the coin had sailed through the first week without any significant problems. He did, however, point out that certain text messages in the client kept appearing and would be fixed in a future upgrade to a new v0.2 protocol. He said the code had already been written for v0.2. It only had to be tested before release in the next week or so. At the end of his first weekly update, Sunny King said:

> "First week total mintage is 3~4 million coins. We thank our supporters for contributing resources to help the network get started. I am an entrepreneurial type as well as an architect/techie, and I understand taking risks deserves matching reward. The mint curve is quite fair in my opinion, as everyone has free choice to participate in the early stages. Have fun and next week!"

Other events in the month of August were:

- Sunny King coined the term "newmint" to mean newly created coins (from staking) which are yet to mature, before becoming available to a client user.

- FuzzyBear and user "NothingG" looked into setting up an exchange for Peercoin.

- Difficulty of the Peercoin network went from 256 to 3,000 in less than three days from the beginning of the launch.

- On the 26th of August at 22:51:11 UTC, the Peercoin subreddit was created at www.reddit.com/r/ppcoin.

- FuzzyBear attempted to create a Windows interface for a future potential wallet client. He was successful in producing his first public program on a Window 7 x64 operating system.

Block #6325

Type:	Proof of Stake
Confirmations:	164053
Size:	2415 bytes
Height:	6325 (Longest chain)
Version:	1
Time:	2012-09-18 22:01:24
Nonce:	0
Bits:	1c00ffff
Difficulty:	256.0
Transactions:	5
Input:	20662.889992 PPC
Output:	20662.839992 PPC
Reward:	2.03 PPC
Fees:	0.05 PPC
Coin age destroyed:	345446.382014 PPC days
Average coin age:	13.447643 days

FIRST PEERCOIN CRYPTOCURRENCY EXCHANGES AND THE FIRST PROOF OF STAKE BLOCK
SEPTEMBER 2012

I.   Sunny King released the official v0.2.0 release build client.

II.   "mugen" created the first Peercoin trading exchange called Cryptocoin.

III.   "doublec" created the second Peercoin trading exchange called Bitparking.

IV.   "dreamwatcher" created the first Peercoin block explorer.

V.   The first proof of stake block was successfully found.

On the first day of September, a Bitcointalk thread was created by Sunny King titled "[ANN] [PPC] PPCoin 0.2.0 Release - Upgrade Required". It announced that a new release build (Version 0.2.0) had been made available for download via the official website www.ppcoin.org. This version included:

- Network protocol upgrade to fix the exception message in debug log.

- Main chain and block generation protocol upgrade to improve security.

- Allow multiple outputs in coinbase and coinstake special transactions.

- Track mint (getblock) and moneysupply (getinfo) figures.

- Public testnet is now up and running.

Sunny King pointed out that this update had achieved most design goals of the Peercoin project, so was a important step forward.

He also said that checkpointing can be gradually weakened and eventually removed (checkpointing from this point was assessed on a monthly basis).

Users had to upgrade to this new version before the 10th of September 2012, otherwise they would have found themselves disconnected from the main Peercoin network. He then advised members of the community on how to backup and safeguard their client files during the switch to v0.2.0.

On the official Peercoin Bitcointalk thread on the 4th of September at 00:46:35 UTC, user "mugen" announced that he had compiled a 0.2.0 beta for a Peercoin exchange called Cryptocoin. Sunny King responded with the comment:

> "Congratulations to mugen and Cryptocoin Exchange being the first to start trading ppcoin :)"

Also, FuzzyBear responded:

> "Gratz mugen and Cryptocoin Exchange... u beat me to it!!"

Also on the 4th, FuzzyBear created a Peercoin wallet for Windows. This software update incorporated the Peercoin coin logo on the user interface as well as the ability to view new coin statistics. Faulty popup windows were also fixed.

Three days later on the 7th of September, user "doublec" (Chris) created the second exchange for trading Peercoin called Bitparking. He was quoted as saying:

> "...and I'll see how it goes as to whether it's a long term thing or not."

On the 9th of September, user "xisalty" had built a Windows GUI client. A user called "Rubberduckie" was quoted as saying:

> "awesome job! Thanks for your hard work :)"

One day later, "xisalty" added the Peercoin icon in addition to changing the naming in the source so the client displayed Peercoin instead of Bitcoin.

On the 10th of September, the Peercoin network switched protocol to version 0.2.0 at 18:00 UTC.

On the 11th of September, user "doublec" (Chris) announced that he had set up a Bitparking mining pool. Also on this day, it was stated that the price of one PPC unit of account was about 0.00015 BTC or 6,500 PPC per BTC.

An important milestone in the blockchain occurred about one week later on the 18th at 22:01:24 UTC. It was the generation of the first proof of stake block at block number 6,325. This took place about thirty days after the initial launch date.

On the 27th of September at 09:40:45 UTC on Bitcointalk, user "cunicula" was quoted as saying:

> "Thanks for doing all the hard work to create this great project.
> However, for the record:
> 1) Proof-of-stake is brought up by "QuantumMechanic" in mid July 2011..."

Sunny King acknowledged this fact and said:

> "I'd give you that you and medi started your designs a couple of months before us. Although we are the first to bring a working design to the market."

Other important events this month were:

- User "dreamwatcher" created the very first Peercoin block explorer on the 18th of September. It was made available at the website http://www.ppcexplore.org:2750/. He made the community aware that bugs were likely to cause the site to malfunction from time to time. One day later, the URL was slightly amended to www.ppcexplore.org (does not exist anymore).

- In the middle of September, an updated client was released (v0.2.1). Users were not required to update to this version as only very minor bugs in the code were fixed.

FIRST NON-EXCHANGE WEBSITE ACCEPTS
PEERCOIN AS PAYMENT

OCTOBER 2012

I.   Sunny King began to publish all weekly updates on one single thread.

II.   Total network money supply surpassed 10 million Peercoin.

III.   The first non-exchange website to accept Peercoin as payment created.

IV.   Block number 10,000 surpassed.

V.   User "liquid" proposed a new Peercoin logo.

Since the 26th of August 2012 at 16:14:04 UTC, Sunny King had posted weekly updates on the main Peercoin thread on Bitcointalk. He had posted weekly updates one to six on there until he made the following announcement on the 2nd of October at 20:49:40 UTC:

> "Due to popular request I would start posting weekly updates to a separate thread with links in the main thread. Thanks!"

This happened as a consequence of the community asking Sunny King to keep all weekly updates separate from the rest of the main Peercoin discussion. One can find the weekly updates, starting at update #7, on the Bitcointalk thread at https://bitcointalk.org/index.php?topic=114994.0.

On the 3rd of October at 00:50:42 UTC, the total number of Peercoin generated since launch had surpassed ten million via both proof of work and proof of stake timestamping methods. This occurred at block number 8,186 at which 1010.46 coins were generated via proof of work mining at that block.

Throughout the middle of October 2012, a growing number of forum users were participating in the discussion about Peercoin. The main topic discussed at this time was the subject of proof of stake. A greater understanding of how proof of stake blocks are generated was highly sought after.

At the same time, user "AndyRossy" publicly thanked user "doublec" for the creation of the Bitparking exchange. Trading volume on this had been in the 100,000s of PPC on a daily basis. Another user called "liquid" was quoted as saying:

> "We need PPC on http://btc-e.com/ :D" … "…and mtgox."

This did partially become a reality. It trades on BTC-e, but never did on Mt Gox.

On the 21st of October, there was a discussion between users "AndyRossy", "liquid" and "dreamwatcher" as to whether a new coin logo should be created. At 12:26:39 UTC, user "AndyRossy" was quoted as saying:

> "Maybe we should put up a bounty, something to make it worth it, like 5 BTC, for a competition winner. If we have maybe 5+ candidates, then we could all vote (for PPC logo obv.)"

User "liquid" proposed a new coin logo at the time, but there is no record of an image. A response by user "dreamwatcher" was made:

> "Is there something wrong with the one we use now?"

User "AndyRossy" replied:

> "Did not say this, but, it's good to get more people involved with PPC in many ways."

Other important events this month were:

- Progress on release build version 0.3.0 was underway. Sunny King made it clear that its release would be delayed due to his own personal circumstances of heavy workload throughout the end of 2012.

- Satoshi Roulette were the first non-exchange website to accept Peercoin as a form of payment in the second week of October. It is a game site.

- On the 15th of October 2012, block number 10,000 was reached at 10:41:39 UTC. It was a proof of stake block with the attributed reward of 1.75 PPC.

VIRCUREX EXCHANGE

NOVEMBER 2012

I.   More proof of stake blocks than proof of work blocks.

II.   Sunny King released the official v0.2.2 release build.

III.   Vircurex added Peercoin to their exchange platform.

IV.   User "xchrix" created the site called www.cryptocoincharts.info.

V.   Bitcoin proof of work mining reward halved from 50 BTC to 25 BTC.

Very little recorded discussion on the official Peercoin Bitcointalk thread took place in the first week or so of November. Only two comments, both from Sunny King, were posted from the 1st to the 10th days of the month on that forum.

One of the main occurrences in the first few days of November concerned proof of stake blocks. Proof of stake blocks now accounted for more than half of all blocks generated. A quote from Sunny King at the time was:

> " It is expected in the next month or two proof-of-stake blocks would reach the 10 minute spacing target and proof-of-stake difficulty should begin rising above the current minimum of 1."

He also made it clear that as the ten minute spacing target of proof of stake block generation is approached in the next month or so, the difficulty of finding a proof of work block will increase. As a result, proof of work blocks will become more sparse in the blockchain. Proof of work spacing target was designed to be variable in the range ten minutes to two hours. Therefore, proof of work spacing tends to two hours as proof of stake becomes more dominant.

On the 10th of November, Sunny King expected v0.2.2 of the release build client to be available in the next week. It would include an improvement to allow users to clearly see their total staked coins and transactions.

On the 14th, Sunny King posted a reply on Bitcointalk showing how Peercoin faired against other cryptocurrencies at the time. He was quoted as saying:

"FYI, ppcoin market cap closing in on devcoin (based on vircurex and bitparking data):

```
currency - estimated current market cap (in BTC)
#1 BTC   - 10,400,000
#2 LTC   -     75,000
#3 NMC   -     18,000
#4 DVC   -      6,580
#5 PPC   -      6,150
#6 IXC   -      1,030
```

Disclaimer: PPC is *experimental* software please be fully aware of investment risks."

In mid November, Sunny King released the official v0.2.2 release build client.

Vircurex (short for Virtual Currency Exchange) was the third cryptocurrency exchange to add Peercoin to their trading platform on the 16th of November 2012. This exchange was founded in October 2011. An opening thread on Bitcointalk states the opening date as the 22nd of October 2011. The opening PPC/BTC value was 0.0005 according to www.cryptocoincharts.info.

*The term "FYI" means "For Your Information" and is used in forum discussions.

Peercoin would not pass this value in terms of Bitcoin on Vircurex again until the 12th of March 2013. The daily trading volume of Peercoin on Vircurex on the first day was about 2,339 PPC.

On the 19th of November, user "xchrix" created a site that displays many historical price charts of a vast array of coins (www.cryptocoincharts.info).

On the 28th of November, the proof of work mining reward generated by miners of the Bitcoin network suddenly halved from 50 BTC to 25 BTC at block number 210,000. Block number 209,999 was successfully found at about 15:01 UTC and the following block at about 15:24 UTC. Sunny King cautioned the Peercoin community about the possible rise in volatility in the price of Peercoin just before and following this event. He was quoted as saying:

> "FYI
> Bitcoin reached 210000th block a moment ago and bitcoin mint rate has halved to 25 btc per block. Coinotron is now showing 1.84 profitability for ppcoin so proof-of-work difficulty is expected to rise from here (currently around 18000).
>
> Congratulations to bitcoin"

On the last day of November at 14:53:18 UTC, forum user "EskimoBob" was quoted as saying:

> "New Difficulty record: 30 130
> Massive jump started on 28/29 when BTC halved and it's mining became close to 2x less profitable than mining PPC and 2.2 x less profitable than LTC."

Also on the last day, the value of one PPC on Vircurex closed at 0.00025008 BTC.

PEERCOIN MINING DIFFICULTY REACHES ALL TIME HIGH FOR THE YEAR 2012

DECEMBER 2012

I.   Peercoin proof of work difficulty increased after BTC halving from 50 to 25.

II.   First Peercoin payment processor created at www.cryptocoinsend.com.

III.   Proof of work difficulty reached an all time high for the year 2012.

IV.   Total network money supply surpassed 15 million PPC.

V.   Release build client v0.3.0 currently on schedule.

When the block reward of Bitcoin halved from fifty to twenty five at block number 210,000 on the 28th of November 2012, there was a big increase in the difficulty of mining Peercoin proof of work blocks. This was understandable considering that the miners suddenly found themselves mining Bitcoin at a certain profit, and then were only being rewarded with half as much. Some miners of Bitcoin were then in a situation of finding a more profitable option, that being Peercoin amongst other coins. As a consequence of this, the Peercoin proof of work difficulty reached a new record of about 30,677 at block number 17,333. The price of Peercoin on Bitparking looked fairly stable during this period after the Bitcoin mining reward halved.

The closing value of one PPC unit of account on Vircurex on the 1st of December was 0.00026 BTC or 0.26 mBTC (1 mBTC = 1/1000th of a Bitcoin).

On the 3rd of December 2012, user "xchrix" created the first website supporting the means for processing payments of Peercoin at www.cryptocoinsend.com. Sunny King at 19:25:09 UTC was quoted as saying:

> "Christian Eisenberg seems to be beta testing at
> http://www.cryptocoinsend.com/ where you can send ppcoin
> (and litecoin) to anybody via email.
>
> Gratz to Christian"

User "xchrix" (aka Christian) replied to this comment:

> "thank you for the mention 😊 its true. unfortunately this week i don't
> have time for this project 😊 too many daywork todo. i will give my
> best! there is also www.cryptocoincharts.info which i made. with some
> PPC charts!"

Cryptocoinsend.com is no longer available.

On the 10th of December, the difficulty of proof of work mining reached a peak of 43,120 at block number 19,080. After this peak had been reached, it would not be until the 17th of March 2013 that a higher figure was surpassed.

On the 15th of December, the total number of PoW and PoS blocks generated since launch reached and surpassed 20,000. User "dreamwatcher" shouted out:

>

Also on this day, user "420" was quoted as saying:

> "why are there over 14 million ppc coins? (more than btc all time) in just
> a few months?"

User "dreamwatcher" responded by saying:

> "POW rewards are different from BTC. POW rewards have been between ~700 to ~2000 coins vs. BTC straight 50 coins (Now 25 coins) per block. If you look at the straight list of blocks
> http://www.cryptocoinexplorer.com:2750/chain/PPcoin
> You will see the vast majority of blocks are now POS which produce MUCH smaller coin-base transactions. Initially all the blocks were POW but as PPC becomes the POS based coin it was meant to be, coin generation drops substantially."

On the 16th of December at 15:29:34 UTC, Sunny King said:

> "Current checkpointing policy is expected to stay at least until the first anniversary or $1M market cap.
>
> If no severe vulnerability is found during the period, checkpointing policy will start to be weakened.
> At some point checkpoint will become optional."

On the 27th of December, the total number of PPC (money supply in circulation) surpassed 15 million.

In Sunny King's last weekly update of 2012, he said the release of v0.3.0 was currently under development and on schedule. A prediction of about three weeks before being made available for download was announced. His lasts words in this weekly update were:

> "Happy New Year to All!"

Vircurex recorded a final closing price of one PPC at 0.000331 BTC and daily volume of about 302.75 PPC on the 31st of December 2012. Sunny King's top priority was to continue to uphold the security and proper operation of the PPCoin network as we were about to enter 2013.

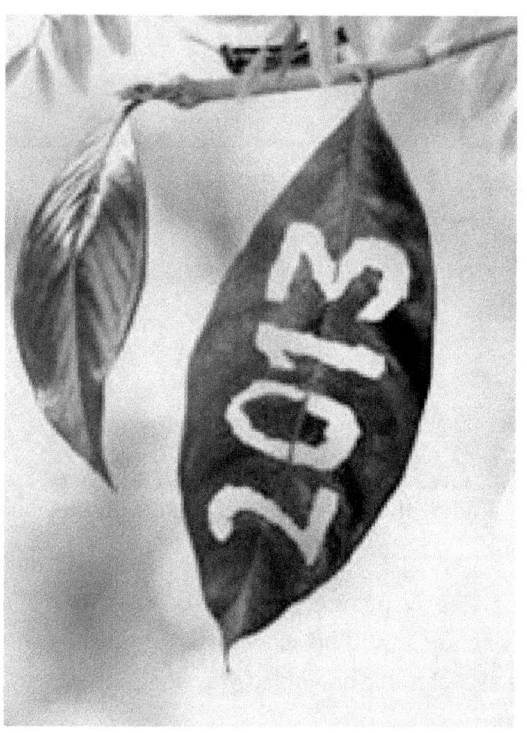

TESTING OF VERSION 0.3.0 OF THE RELEASE BUILD

JANUARY 2013

I.   Version 0.3.0 was about 80% code completed within the first week of 2013.

II.   A prediction of release of v0.3.0 at the end of January.

III.   Price of PPC fell about 49% in terms of BTC from start to end of the month.

IV.   Sunny King and "Jutarul" misunderstanding.

V.   Version 0.3.0 code completed.

Peercoin entered the new year of 2013 with much promise and optimism. Very little announced community activity occurred except for the continued testing of a future build release (version 0.3.0).

In the first week of 2013, Sunny King announced that the code of the future build release of the client was 80% complete. He highlighted the fact that the new code was under some preliminary testing and needed about one to two weeks further time to make sure the current testing would be of high quality. He made a prediction of the release at the end of January.

In his twenty first Peercoin weekly update on the 15th of January, Sunny King announced that version 0.3 was 90% complete besides the first round of testing. He reiterated the importance of going through thorough testing for as long as necessary so as to avoid potential flaws and pitfalls which would otherwise arise.

On the 18th of January, Sunny King was quoted as saying:

> "Market is in some sort of 'crash' mode for the day, bitparking has volume over 1.5m as of now, meaning more than 10% of the total ppcoin changed hands today.
>
> On one hand it shows healthy depth of the market, but this drop does feel somewhat abnormal. I will be monitoring the network closely in the next few days.
>
> If you notice any abnormal events on the network please let me know."

Also on the 18th, Sunny King said:

> "It's probably some early investors lose interest or feel uncertain about the 0.3 protocol upgrade. I'd say that the work is making good progress and will be released soon."

One user of Bitcointalk blamed the ~20% decrease in the PPC/BTC exchange rate on Sunny King's reference to future potential volatility before this decrease. Nevertheless, it was expected that the market would suffer from high volatility in its early stages due to such a small market plus a small number of investors with substantial amounts of money invested. Also in the month of January, another user called "Jutarul" was quoted as saying:

> "By openly criticizing you for the few things which go wrong, I give you a chance to explain to the community why you do things a certain way."

This statement was in response to a misunderstanding between Sunny and "Jutarul". Jutarul said that uncertainly was being manufactured. Sunny King took this personally. This was resolved in a matter of hours.

After continuous testing and finding of bugs in the new code, the code of 0.3 was announced as completed on the 28th of January. Testing of the protocol switch had also begun on testnet. With time permitting, he also eluded to the possibility of starting to look into a QT wallet client for the release.

On Vircurex, the price of one PPC in terms of Bitcoin closed at 0.00017999 BTC on the 31st of January 2013.

Below was the first block of 2013:

Block Height: 22707		Block Time: 2013-01-01 00:11:48 UTC
Block Version	**Block Size**	**Mint Value**
proof-of-stake	917	0.66
Block Bits	**Block Nonce**	**Block Difficulty**
1d00a965	0	1.51124178
Merkle Root	efd5d9074ad9262dda7f4bb1fd006fa083a3de0383f62b6c124fbf2ce68b1f05	
Block Hash	8ce06f7c22ef7d1883045910484c9b8d6364e1e768906c5b98928ddf643e5ab3	

RELEASE OF VERSION 0.3.0 BUILD, QT CLIENT AND
THE FIRST PEERCOIN FORK CALLED NOVACOIN

FEBRUARY 2013

I.   Continued testing of the official 0.3.0 build release (on testnet).

II.   First Peercoin fork called Novacoin launched.

III. Sunny King released the official 0.3.0 release build and qt client.

IV.   "smoothie" dissatisfaction with developer communication.

V.   "Past and Present Alternatives to Bitcoin" article.

The month began with further testing of the future build release v0.3.0 on testnet (a test network used to run the new code and to find whether it will work properly once released). In the first two weeks of February, it was announced:

- Users "Andy" and "xchris" helped to test the new upcoming protocol.

- No significant flaws or errors were found in the testing. The system on testnet reached a stable state.

- Development of a Windows qt client was successful. It would be available.

- On the 11th of February, Sunny King, in his #25 weekly update, stated the current testing would last one further week. After this, the release would occur.

Also in early February, the first ASIC miner was delivered to the market.

On the 9th of February 2013, the first fork of Peercoin called Novacoin was launched. Sunny King said clearly that he was not involved in Novacoin in any way, but he was happy to see other developers valuing the code/design of Peercoin.

On the 11th of February, Sunny King was quoted on the official Novacoin Bitcointalk thread as saying:

"Well congratulations to the first running ppcoin fork 😊 Okay I am a bit surprised but happy 😊 I think forks are endorsements of the value of our work and I don't mind more competition" 🛐

NOVACOIN SPECIFICATION SUMMARY

Date of Genesis Block:	5th of February 2013 at 22:56:57 UTC
Date of Launch:	9th of February 2013 at 16:21:22 UTC
Symbol:	NVC
Founder:	Balthazar
Hashing Algorithm:	Scrypt
Timestamping Alogorithm:	Proof of Work/Proof of Stake

On the 18th of February, after final preparations and validations of the new code were complete, it was announced by Sunny King that v0.3 would be ready in the next few days. He made this announcement in his 26th weekly update. However, the release occurred less than twenty hours after this announcement at about 11:50 PM UTC. It was based on bitcoin v0.6.3. Sunny King at the time said:

"0.3.0 Released!
https://bitcointalk.org/index.php?topic=144964.0
Cheers!"

This update of the code had to be downloaded and installed by users by the 20th of March 2013. Besides the release build, a qt client was also made available.

On the 19th of February, a short discussion between Sunny King and "smoothie" occurred on the official Peercoin Bitcointalk thread. This was in response to the release of version 0.3.0. "smoothie" began with the reply:

"You really need to disclose the new POS algorithm publicly.
I'll eventually get around to looking through the code but you may as well open up the discussion.
I mean, seriously, what is there to hide? You've been very quiet when it comes to discussing this particular topic in detail.
Why is that?"

Sunny King replied to the above by saying:

"Smoothie, there is nothing to hide. I already discussed in my weekly updates thread a couple of weeks ago the general outline of it. If you are interested in studying it why don't you get started with the source code and then post intelligent questions in my disclosure thread for discussion?"

"smoothie" replied:

"I beg to differ. You briefly mentioned using previous block hashes to determine new POS hash. That doesn't really say much.
But okay I will take a look at the code and as I am sure others will be looking at it as well.
To be honest, I'm not sure why you are forcing people to look only at the code as opposed to publicly disclosing your algorithm. Satoshi didn't have a problem with disclosing his...not sure why you would...but okay have it your way."

The final reply made by Sunny King in response to "smoothie" was:

> "To be honest with you I already did quite a bit extra work writing comments in the code to help readers. As a developer I have a lot of different priorities you need to understand. If you mean writing another white paper for this currently I have no plan of doing it.
>
> My next focus is in supporting database usage in ppcoin. But I will follow up with short explanations if there is enough interest in discussing the new algorithm."

On the 23rd of February 2013, Sunny King said:

> "A good couple of months for me. I am relieved that 0.3 is finally done. And I also enjoy watching all the new projects going on like ripple and novacoin."

On the 24th of February 2013, an article was published by John Vandivier titled "Past and Present Alternatives to Bitcoin". In the article, a segment was written about PPCoin. This was:

> "As a matter of theory many current monetary thinkers, especially in the Austrian school of economics or those involved in the bleeding edge of technology including Bitcoin, have long anticipated competition to Bitcoin. We see the competition as good and healthy in the long term because competition usually fosters quality over time. This article will not analyze current Bitcoin alternatives in-depth, but it will list and briefly summarize those alternatives, noting some advantages and drawbacks.
>
> 5) PPCoin. A largely abandoned project which was poorly done but a great idea. The idea is to copy Bitcoin but replace the Proof of Work system Bitcoin does with a Proof of Stake system. Proof of Stake can do the same essential job of Proof of Work with only a sliver of the time and energy required by an intense Proof of Work. In this forum post Sunny King, one of the PPCoin makers, says that Ripple could accomplish the same essential advantage of PPCoin."

As the last post for February 2013 on the official Peercoin Bitcointalk thread, Sunny King responded to the article. He said:

"Thanks John for the compliments to ppcoin project. However I'd like to point out that ppcoin is neither 'largely abandoned' nor 'poorly done'.

Yes I said ripple could potentially accomplish the energy efficiency goal as well. However the tradeoff appears to be very different. We must keep in mind that ripple in the current state is still practically centralized, with only a few validation nodes all controlled by OpenCoin. For ppcoin even though the level of decentralization is lower than that of bitcoin, for the protection of initial bootstrapping of the network, the degree of decentralization is still a lot higher than ripple as of now. Ripple's design is still far from tested as to its robustness and ability to decentralize. There is operating concerns as well regarding how many such ripple validation nodes would eventually be maintained by public since there is no clear incentive for people to do so. Also unlike ripple, ppcoin was released without any centralized issurance (that's why ppcoin kept proof-of-work). The risk profiles of the two projects are very different, both technically and politically.

Having said that, I do appreciate the work of ripple team and it's ambitions in alternative credit system (basically a return to free banking on Internet). Clearly the team behind ripple is very resourceful and brave. I sincerely wish them good luck.

But people should not interpret it as if I have 'abandoned' ppcoin project. Having just released 0.3 protocol upgrade, my long term plan is to enable database use with ppcoin. If you'd like to hear my opinion, I think ppcoin project is well-alive and promising. I feel I have it in me to contribute a lot more to the world of cryptocurrency in the future."

On the 28th of February, the closing Vircurex price of one PPC unit of account was 0.000092 BTC. This was a decrease in value from the closing value on the first day of the month at 0.00013306 BTC. After about three and a half months, there were still only three exchanges actively trading in Peercoin. Could the next few months see other exchanges trading it?

SWITCH TO VERSION 0.3.0 AND A NEW OFFICIAL PEERCOIN CHAT FORUM

MARCH 2013

I.   Coin faucet became available via the official website www.ppcoin.org

II.   Sunny King invited to the Bitcoin Foundation.

III.   Protocol switched to the official v0.3.0 release build.

IV.   New Peercoin Official Forum created at www.peercointalk.org.

V.   Peercoin added to Biticker Chrome App.

In terms of market capitalisation, Peercoin was now neck and neck with Devcoin. Accordingly to the comments made by Sunny King in his weekly update (#28) on the 3rd of March 2013, many people in the cryptocurrency space were putting their faith in scrypt coins such as Litecoin and Novacoin. This was evident with these two possessing much higher market capitalisations.

Since the release of v0.3.0, many announcements were made that the network continued to function properly. Sunny King also reminded users to update to this new version before the 20th March, the date on which the protocol switched.

On the 6th of March, Sunny King replied to a couple of comments which labelled Peercoin as having no infrastructure, future or sustainability. He emphasised that he would continue to work hard to make the coin a success. Members of the community now started to use the term Peercoin more often instead of PPCoin.

He reminded people not to invest more than they can afford to lose considering the risk and volatility attributed to the Peercoin market at the time. He considers Peercoin as one of his best works in his career.

Other events that occurred in the first two weeks of March 2013 were:

- A faucet was created by Sunny King available via ppcoin.org.

- A Peercoin public/private key generator compatible with version 0.3.0 was also created by Sunny King at www.ppcoin.org/bitaddress. At the start it was subject to public testing.

- Sunny King received an invitation from the Bitcoin Foundation to attend a panel on altcoins at the May 2013 Conference in California, USA. He told the Peercoin community of his inability to attend the event, however he would help a volunteer who could. (http://www.bitcoin2013.com)

On the 14th of March, user "sangaman" at 17:38:36 UTC was quoted as saying:

> "Is there any update on when we can expect PPC to move off check pointing? It will be a big step forward."

"sangaman" also brought up the recurring issue of changing the name of the coin and redesigning the official website to make it look simpler, cleaner and more presentable. He offered to contribute his time towards making this possible. He suggested holding a public vote and renaming the coin to ECoin. Sunny King replied to this suggestion by saying:

> "I am sorry regarding the name I already said it should be as it is, so let's move on. As for checkpoint, I am not in a hurry to weaken it as it was the mechanism to defend the last known vulnerability. Eventually it would become not enforced but only advisory. But we are still far from there in my opinion."

On the 19th of March, FuzzyBear created a new official Peercoin chat forum on which a more professional, organised and managed conversation about the coin could occur. The second topic recorded on the forum is the following comment made by FuzzyBear at 00:50:20 UTC on the same day:

> "Hey all finally got a better forum for PPCoin sorted out 😊 most should all be more familiar with this. Feel free to sign up , I will be moving the URL to http://www.ppcointalk.org but that will not change the users created on here.http://new.ppcointalk.org
> I will leave the old site up until I move the content across, sorry but I don't think it will be possible to port the user accounts across.
> Let me know of any bug or suggestions and have fun with your PPCoins!"

On the 20th of March, the Peercoin network successfully switched to v0.3.0.

Other events in the month were:

- Facebook group created on the 4th of March at www.facebook.com/PPcoin.

- A Biticker (a free chrome extension) began supporting Peercoin on the 28th of March at https://chrome.google.com/webstore/.

- A slide was published in Ron Gross's presentation on altcoin technologies on the 27th of March (see opposite)

According to Vircurex, the price of one PPC unit of account in terms of BTC closed at 0.0002541 BTC on the 31st of March. It had closed at 0.00008696 BTC on the first day of the month. This was an increase of approximately 292%. Would the month of April beat this increase?

http://www.slideshare.net/ripper234/alternative-payment-technologies-march-2013

MARKET CAPITALISATION SURGE

APRIL 2013

I.   Bitparking exchange closed.

II.   Market capitalisation surged over $8 million.

III.   BTC-e and Bter began to trade Peercoin on their exchanges.

IV.   Holy Angels Church was the first charitable organisation to accept Peercoin.

V.   Direct Voltage was the first retailer to accept Peercoin as payment.

At the beginning of April, Sunny King had written a page on the Peercoin wiki titled "History of Cryptocurrency" and had linked a wallet generator to the main official Peercoin website. He had also helped Novacoin and Freicoin with network protocol issues. In early April, Sunny King was quoted as saying:

"There seems to be lots of confusion regarding whether ppcoin is more inflationary than bitcoin. So I have updated the wiki FAQ section on money supply to be (hopefully) easier to understand for new users. As I have already indicated in the design paper, we recognize the importance of scarcity in a free-market currency. No we do not subscribe to ~Keynesian economyics. I generally agree with Satoshi's view in this matter, and I also recognize the immutability of minting model of a serious cryptocurrency."

On the 4th of April 2013 at 14:17:37 UTC, user "coinotron" was quoted as saying:

> "Sunny King, do you have plans to introduce new stuff from bitcoin 0.8 i.e. getblocktemplate, getrawtransactions etc ?"

Sunny King replied by saying:

> "Yes bitcoin 0.8 features are planned for next release."

On the 5th of April 2013 at 01:45:10 UTC, Sunny King said:

> "I try to help all altcoins irregardless whether I like them or not myself, yeah even for novacoin which is a fork of ppcoin, I know many other people would outright hate copycat projects of their creation but I have a different mindset. I think many of us don't yet realize that even though we are competing against each other in the market, we are really all part of a big team leading the world into a new era."

Also on the 5th of April, the Bitparking exchange closed at about 22:00 UTC. User "doublec" said he found running the exchange too risky and stressful for him personally due to the high price Peercoin had attained. He encouraged users of the exchange to use Vircurex instead and made it easy for people to withdraw their funds without the usual fees. The exchange had been operational for two hundred and ten days. Sunny King responded to the closure by saying:

> "Due to steep rise of the market Chris has now closed his bitparking exchange and pool. I would like to express my sincere gratitude to Chris for all his hard work and professionalism since ppcoin's release. Bitparking was the first active exchange market for ppcoin which played a major role in jump-starting ppcoin market. Chris said it was more like a hobby level project, but actually he was being very modest. My experience is that bitparking exchanges were managed with high degree of professionalism and integrity.
> I am looking forward to Chris's next projects."

On the following day, a new exchange called BTC-e added the trading pair PPC/BTC to their platform. BTC-e was first announced on the 17th of July 2011 in test mode. It initiated live trading on the 7th of August 2011. At the time of publication of this book, it is one of the mayor cryptocurrency exchanges in existence. According to the site www.cryptocoincharts.info, the opening value of one PPC unit of account in terms of Bitcoin was 0.003 BTC. Its high for the same day was 0.00349 BTC. The respective total daily trading volume was about 631,271 PPC. BTC-e was the fourth exchange to add Peercoin, but had become, as a result of the Bitparking closure and inactivity of Cryptocoin, the second actively trading exchange alongside Vircurex.

The first week of April also saw massive gains in the price of Peercoin. In his weekly update (#33) on the 8th of April, Sunny King was quoted as saying:

> "What a week! PPCoin has achieved multiple milestones in the cryptocurrency market this week.
>
> Market cap surpassed namecoin and now ranked behind litecoin at 50,000 BTC or over $8M as of today, or about 0.5% of bitcoin and over 10% of litecoin.
>
> Proof-of-work difficulty continued to break all time high throughout the week and is now at 280,000 as of today."

On the first day of the month, the opening Bitcoin price of one PPC was 0.00023001 BTC on Vircurex. By the 8th of April, the price reached a local peak of 0.00292 BTC, an increase of approximately 12.69 fold (1169% increase) in the space of about eight days. BTC-e recorded a larger high of 0.00302 BTC per PPC on the same day.

Surprisingly, the 8th of April was not the day on which Peercoin reached its all time high before the 19th of August 2013. The fiat value of Bitcoin in dollar terms continued to rise higher over the next two days at a higher rate than the fall in the Peercoin exchange value in Bitcoin terms. According to sites such as www.bitinfocharts.com and www.cryptocoincharts.info, the market capitalisation peaked on the 9th of April at about $8.08 million. The highs on exchanges were:

- Vircurex—   0.00265 BTC per PPC

- BTC-e—   0.0026 BTC per PPC

The average value of one Peercoin was about $0.44 on the 9th of April.

On the 10th of April, the value of one Bitcoin reached a peak of $266, and then dropped down to nearly $100 in a matter of hours. At the beginning of 2013, the value of one Bitcoin was $13. An article was written by Vitalik Buterin titled "The Bitcoin Crash: An Examination" at the link:

https://bitcoinmagazine.com/4113/the-bitcoin-crash-an-examination/

On the 15th of April, an article titled "Bitcoin Isn't the Only Cryptocurrency in Town" was written by Tom Simonite. In reference to what was said about Peercoin:

"PPCoin's design is intended to gradually phase out conventional mining alto-gether. Instead of new PPCoins being handed out to those with the most computational muscle, they are awarded in a kind of lottery in which a miner's chance of winning is determined by how many PPCoins they have.

That has the effect of decoupling mining and the confirmation of transactions from the cost of electricity and computer power, which King says would be a problem for Bitcoin if it were to become very widely used. "We designed PPCoin with this new concept to achieve long-term energy efficiency," says Sunny King, one of the founders of PPCoin. "This will not only provide environmental benefit, but also allow us to be more cost-competitive in payment processing."

"A complete monopoly in the cryptocurrency world is unlikely," says King, of PPCoin, "I am optimistic that payment processing in cryptocurrency will take over a significant portion of Internet commerce.""

Peercoin was now the fourth ranked cryptocurrency in terms of market capitalisation behind Bitcoin, Ripple and Litecoin. It had managed to surpass Namecoin above which it had remained on the 15th of April 2013.

On the 18th of April 2013 at 20:55:16 UTC, user "cosmoo" was quoted as saying:

"i'm not a developer but i find your attitude infectious Sunny, especially in seeing what cryptocurrencies can really accomplish. i hope your efforts in this affect all of us (and they already are!) thank you for your work!

you have a great mind that's well taken care of 😵 i have enjoyed reading your posts."

Sunny King replied to this compliment:

"Thanks for the compliment 😵 Satoshi's work inspires me and I hope

my work could inspire more people to join the exciting new field" 😵

On the 22nd of April at 00:24:43 UTC, Sunny King posted his first comment on the official Peercointalk forum. His opening statement was:

"Dear supporters of ppcoin project,

First I'd like to thank FuzzyBear for his hard work of hosting this nice forum. As you know that bitcointalk's altcoin forum is getting very crowded these days with different altcoins it becomes more and more difficult to follow ppcoin threads there. So as we gain more popularity I will begin to visit this forum more often.

As you probably already know, that we are among the very few cryptocurrency projects that actually attempt at real innovations, rather than just cloning bitcoin and making some small tweaks. I believe the future of cryptocurrency to be a very competitive market, with multiple major currencies of different designs. We are still a fairly young project, most people still don't know about our innovations and cannot distinguish us from all the clone altcoins. This is where our supporters can join forces and help the community grow, by raising awareness in the cryptocurrency market about the benefit of continued innovation in this field and the need to support real innovations."

> I would like to also thank our supporters for your personal encouragements to me, it means a lot to me. We must remember what the cryptocurrency movement represents to humanity, a return of monetary power back to the free market, an upgraded guard of private property, one of the pillars of human civilization. Armed with this new advancement, liberty now has a better chance. I am so happy there are people out there sharing the same view with me, so that I know I am not alone walking the path, and together we will gain more courage, help each other, and make the history.
>
> Welcome to the forum!"

Bter.com listed Peercoin for trading on their exchange on the 24th of April 2013. It was the fifth cryptocurrency exchange to add Peercoin and is an exchange based in China.

Other events in the month of April were:

- Directvoltage.com was the first retailer to accept Peercoin as a form of payment on their website on the 22nd of April 2013.

- Also, to encourage more retail acceptance of Peercoin, a bounty project was opened to promote it to online retailers.

- Holy Angels Church in Chicago USA (holyangels.com) became the first charitable organization to accept Peercoin donations.

- AnonPaste (anonpaste.me) started accepting Peercoin donations.

The month of April saw the all time Bitcoin highs of Peercoin on the exchanges Vircurex, BTC-e and Bter before the 19th of August 2013. It would not be until the 4th of October 2013 that these Bitcoin values were surpassed. These were:

- On the 20th of April, Vircurex reached a high of 0.00329 BTC per PPC.

- On the 26th of April, Bter reached a high of 0.0033 BTC per PPC.

- On the 28th of April, BTC-e reached a high of 0.00339 BTC per PPC.

At the end of the month of April, discussions were held about changing the name of the coin yet again. Users "Yurizhai" and "JessicaMILFson" tried to persuade Sunny King that a name change would be beneficial. Sunny King on the 30th of April 2013 at 04:01:47 UTC was quoted as saying :

"Ok I have heard enough of complaints of the project name. I understand most of you are wishing the project well, but you have to understand, rebranding is not a risk-free task and could cause a lot of confusion in the market, not to mention costing a ton of resources of the project.

Honestly I don't think the name is too bad, it's easy to remember. Yes there are a lot of immature people making fun of the name, but why can't we just ignore them and move on, I believe one day they would be the one looking funny when talking like that.

If you truly believe the name is causing us to lose market, I'd say the evidence is to the contrary. Just one month ago we were still in a close match with devcoin, terracoin, novacoin etc. Apparently the market has decided the name was either not that bad or didn't matter and now we are #3 even ahead of namecoin.

Like I said, if you hate the name with a passion, you can refer it as peercoin as you like. Amidst all these complaints I am a bit surprised to find someone who said ppcoin is a good marketing name, while feathercoin is not, because peer-to-peer is a tech term a lot of people can associate to.

As to our marketing message of energy efficiency, that's why the leaf coin icon was made. Yes it is our central marketing message from the beginning. But I think, peer-to-peer (i.e. decentralization) is the main innovation of cryptocurrency, having it in the name shouldn't be such a bad thing."

CRYPTSY EXCHANGE AND THE THREE FORKS
MAY 2013

I.   Proposed potential Peercoin logos designed.

II.   Bitbar, Yacoin and Bitgem forks of Peercoin launched.

III.   Discussion about improvements to the official website design and layout.

IV.   Exchanges Cryptsy and Crypto Trade add Peercoin to their platforms.

V.   Discussion about transferring more of Peercoin chat to peercointalk.org.

On the second day of May, a new subreddit (www.reddit.com/r/peercoin) was created at 00:28 UTC. There was already a subreddit (.../ppcoin) active, but the community were shifting away from PPCoin as the coin name to Peercoin instead. Also on this day, the second coin forked from the source code of Peercoin was released called Bitbar, BTB. It was released as a Scrypt hashing coin with hybrid proof of work and proof of stake timestamping.

Sunny King, in response to launch of Bitbar, was quoted was saying:

> "In my opinion that's a good thing for ppcoin.
> There will be a lot more clone altcoins by the end of the year. Having multiple clones of our work actually indicates that more developers are valuing the design, and more new users would have opportunity to learn about the original work in ppcoin."

BITBAR SPECIFICATION SUMMARY

Date of Genesis Block:	1st of May 2013 at 22:00:00 UTC
Date of Launch:	2nd of May 2013 at 13:56:10 UTC
Symbol:	BTB
Founder:	Marko Kaasila
Hashing Algorithm:	Scrypt
Timestamping Alogorithm:	Proof of Work/Proof of Stake

Since the very first day of the month, the Peercoin community on Bitcointalk began to suggest designs for a new Peercoin logo. A Bitcointalk user called "Mjbmonetarymetals" created a new thread on this Peercoin logo concept at https://bitcointalk.org/index.php?topic=192741.0

Design by "robotrebellion" on the 1st of May 2013 at 03:53:32 UTC

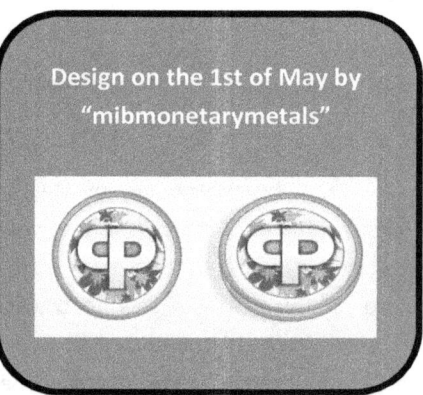

Design on the 1st of May by "mibmonetarymetals"

Sunny King was quoted as saying:

"Thanks to robotrebellion and Mjbmonetarymetals for contribution of graphics work 😊 Oh and a new term 'eco-currency'" 😁

Further coin logo designs courtesy of user "detail3" were published for the community to consider. These are shown below. On the 6th of May at 01:18:34 UTC, he was quoted as saying :

"I've had some professional designers working on this project actually, here is where their designs stand...any input that I can forward on to them would be helpful. As I've said elsewhere, I didn't make these, so feel free to bash them as you will, but constructive criticism is best."

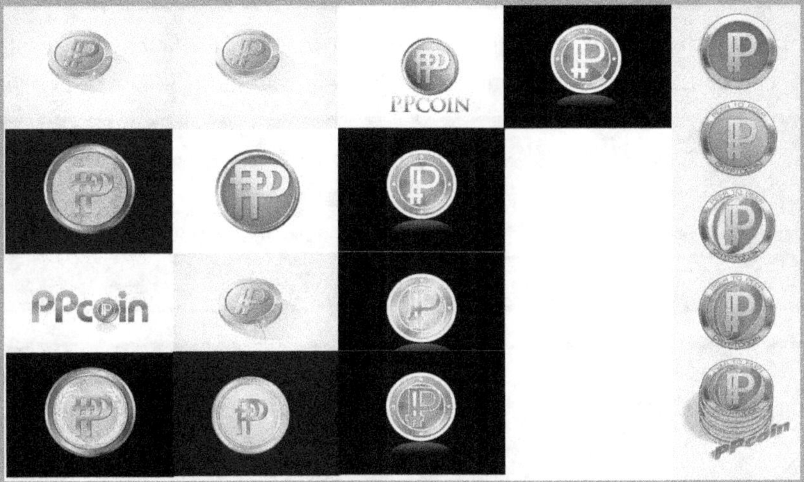

On the 3rd of May at 00:41:40 UTC, Sentinelrv posted his first reply on the official Peercoin Bitcointalk forum thread. He said:

"I've been waiting since last night to post this, since I was relegated to the newbie forum, but I love the new logo, if that is indeed what we're sticking with. I made it my new avatar. I think it helps bring PeerCoin a little more credibility. I just wish the website was updated now to be more friendly and informative to new people."

On the 8th of May, Sentinelrv proposed a new potential Peercoin logo:

> "Here, I altered the design just a little bit to connect the two P's at the top and in the middle so it doesn't look like it says IP anymore. What do you think? I actually like the P symbol more now that it's squished closer together. It looks better than the spaced out version we were working with."

Also on the 8th of May, the third forked coin of Peercoin lauched. Yacoin was announced on the Bitcointalk forum three days earlier. Sunny King's response was:

> "Good. I welcome the 3rd PPC fork that at least tries something slightly different. Dynamic scrypt parameter was something dreamwatcher wanted to do some time ago, I am sure he would be happy to add to his explorer collections"

YACOIN SPECIFICATION SUMMARY

Date of Genesis Block:	8th of May 2013 at 05:33:40 UTC
Date of Launch:	8th of May 2013 at 06:49:33UTC
Symbol:	YAC
Founder:	pocopoco
Hashing Algorithm:	SHA-3/Keccak-512
Timestamping Alogorithm:	Proof of Work/Proof of Stake

Besides the new proposed coin logos, the community was also helping to design new layouts of the official Peercoin website. User "Mibmonetarymetals" said:

> "Excellent, it would be a great start on the road to improving pp.org it shouldn't continue the way it currently looks for much longer as its not to be taken seriously in its current format."

As can be seen above, one potential design was proposed as an alternative to the current official website layout at the top. It would not be until later on that a more professional website became available to the Peercoin community.

In the middle of May, a discussion about which forum would best suit Peercoin was held. There were people who wanted the conversation about the coin to fully shift towards the official Peercoin forum at www.peercointalk.org. Others pointed out that having the conversation on both Bitcointalk and Peercointalk is important.

On the 14th of May at 13:49:11 UTC, user "Excelsior" was quoted as saying:

> "5) ALL of use completely dropping out of bitcointalk and carrying on our conversation at ppcointalk.org, each of us leaving on all ppcoin threads something like the following
> "THIS THREAD IS MOVED TO PPCOINTALK.ORG—JOINS US.""

On the 15th of May at 01:22:52 UTC, Sentinelrv replied to the comments regarding where Peercoin related material should be discussed:

> "Yeah, I'm with Irishmick on this one. I will use ppcointalk, but we need to keep this thread open because it's our main connection to the Bitcoin community. We're not strong enough yet to completely separate ourselves from this forum. This thread acts as an advertisement for ppcoin.
> I would make the suggestion to Sunny to add a link to the first post of this thread to ppcointalk.org, that way we can also use this thread as an advertisement for the new forum. He should also probably link to it from the main website, rather than bitcointalk's alt-coin forum. This will help to build up the community."

Since the launch of the official Peercoin forum at www.peercointalk.org, discussion about the coin was now more frequent there. One day later, the fourth forked coin of Peercoin was launched called Bitgem.

BITGEM SPECIFICATION SUMMARY

Date of Genesis Block:	16th of May 2013 at 07:46:36 UTC
Date of Launch:	16th of May 2013 at 09:26:24 UTC
Symbol:	BTG
Founder:	Mineral
Hashing Algorithm:	Scrypt
Timestamping Alogorithm:	Proof of Work/Proof of Stake

On the 17th of May at 03:42:04 UTC, Sunny King was quoted as saying:

> "Home page forum link will be updated to point to ppcointalk.org soon. Due to the flood of new altcoins directing new ppcoin user to this forum is confusing to say the least.
> However I will continue to put my 80% forum time here because this is an important forum to communicate ppcoin's message and innovations, to a broader audience with interests in cryptocurrency in general."

On the 21st of May, the forum link on the official Peercoin site was made to re-direct to peercointalk.org. On the following day, Peercoin tipping went live on Reddit alongside other coins such as Litecoin, Namecoin, Novacoin and Terracoin.

Cryptsy was the sixth exchange to add Peercoin on the 23rd of May. This was about three days after the launch of the exchange. It is based in Delray Beach, Florida, USA. It has become one of the most reputable cryptocurrency trading exchanges.

After a request by Peercointalk user "d5000" to add a marketplace section to allow the offering of goods or services in Peercoin on the 14th of May, FuzzyBear added the section on the 27th of May. User "d5000" thanked FuzzyBear by saying:

> "Thank you!
> I think the mods should move now the goods/services oriented threads (for example the Jewelry thread) from the Trading and Exchanges forum to the new marketplace, so it doesn't look so empty.
> When I have to sell something,
> I will announce it in the marketplace."

On the 28th of May, Peercoin was added to the trading exchange called Crypto Trade. It opened with a trading value of 0.0015 BTC per PPC with daily trading volume on the first day of exactly 2 PPC. It has since closed down.

On the last day of the month, 0.00127296 BTC, 0.00125 BTC, 0.00159 and 0.00124 BTC were the recorded closing values of one PPC on the exchanges Vircurex, BTC-e, Bter and Cryptsy respectively. The PPC price had fallen during the month of May.

99DESIGNS COIN LOGO DESIGN CONTEST

JUNE 2013

I.   Ppcoin.org marketplace goes live.

II.   Goal of $300 raised for "Bronze Package" on 99designs.

III.   Coins-e exchange began Peercoin trading.

IV.   Logo Design Contest began on 99Designs.

V.   Sunny King pre-announced a future cryptocurrency called Primecoin.

On the second day of June, a YouTube video was published by Jason Schaumleffel. He described the characteristics of Peercoin as well as giving his own opinions on the coin (https://www.youtube.com/watch?v=ynwz8H66chY).

On the 3rd of June, Sunny King created an online Peercoin marketplace. It was originally set up to support Bitcointalk forum accounts. This marketplace was intended to encourage users to trade using PPC as a currency with other coins such as Bitgem and Primecoin. As of 2015, the link to the marketplace at (http://ppcoin.org/market) only redirects to the official website.

On the 6th of June, Sentinelrv made an announcement about how the community would go forward in order to choose the design of the new coin logo. He made reference to the Peercointalk.org thread http://www.ppcointalk.org/index.php?topic=92.0 created on 1st of May consisting for proposed designs.

To move forward, a site called 99designs was chosen as a means to have a logo design contest. It is a site that allows people to offer cash for others to create designs. The "gold package" (cost ~$800) was chosen initially so as to give the greatest exposure of submissions in addition to a future poll option to chose the best design. A donation site was also registered at gofundme.com at http:/ www.gofundme.comppcoinlogodesignfund. Sentinelrv said that once the logo design had been finalised, work could then fully begin on the professional redesigning the official website so as to optimise the marketing of Peercoin.

On the 7th of June, Sunny King asked the Peercoin community to visit the link at https://support.mtgox.com/entries/21676064-Please-Add-Peer-2-Peer-Coin-PPC- in order to help consider PPC trading on the largest crypto exchange in the world. He said it would help greatly to increase the liquidity of PPC.

On the same day, a thread on peercointalk.org was created titled "Peercoin Logo Design Contest Fundraising Thread" (http://www.peercointalk.org/index.php? topic=241.0). Subsequently, the community was encouraged to spread the news of this fund raising campaign on Facebook, Twitter, Reddit and other sites such as exchange chat boxes.

On the 13th of June, the funding goal was reduced from the initial goal of $800 to $300. The reason behind this was that the "bronze package" was viewed as being sufficient to achieve the required goals. No deadline for the funding was in place. Thanks to Peercointalk user "whifmio", the total of $300 was reached on the 18th of June. FuzzyBear on the 19th of June commented:

> "Nice work here everyone especially Sentinelrv and serious
>
> congratulations on raising the funding 😊 Lets keep the ball rolling, so what is the next stage? maybe you want to outline this in the OP or a new thread.... feel free to make it a sticky thread or ask me or an admin to do this if you can not.
>
> FuzzyBear"

Before the $300 target had been achieved, user "super3" posted a question:

> "The website really needs work... Is a new one underway? If not I can put something together if it will actually get used."

Sentinelrv reiterated that any new development of the official website would have to wait until the coin logo had been redesigned. He was quoted as saying:

> "We've been trying to raise $300 to finish off the logo with a design contest. Once that's done we can build a new website around the design of the logo, but it's been slow going in raising the money. We're currently at $95 and Reddit won't let me post about it to gain exposure. That's why I wanted to know if Sunny controlled that ppcoin Facebook page I posted above. That page could post about it to try and finish off the meter. If you or anyone else you know would like to donate to get this finished, here is the link... http://www.gofundme.com/ppcoinlogodesignfund"

On the 20th of June, a new thread at peercointalk.org was created, again by Sentinelrv, titled "Peercoin Logo Design Contest Planning Thread". His opening comment on there was directed towards users who were interested in setting up a new logo design on 99designs and on how to go about it. He also gave his opinions on the design criteria such as the colour scheme and the values the coin should communicate. Sunny King responded early on in this thread by saying:

> "Thanks for organizing the project
> Preferred theme:
> environmental friendly + gold (gold color can be decorations only)
> Please don't use silver/copper, unlike ltc our marketing message Is *not* silver/copper to someone else's gold.
> Currency symbol:
> Official symbol is P with an extra vertical bar (to make it look like 2 P's stacked) with a horizontal bar connecting them.
> It symbolizes peer-to-peer."

On the 22nd of June, Coins-e became the last cryptocurrency trading exchange to add Peercoin before the 19th of August 2013. It was also the opening day of the exchange on which Peercoin made its debut besides about fifteen other coins.

On the 27th of June at 19:16:17 UTC, Sentinelrv made an announcement regarding the 99Designs coin logo contest. He said:

> "The logo design contest is now up at 99designs. I need everyone here to help give feedback to the designers on what you want to see. Feedback is very important in getting a great design. I've setup a thread over at ppcointalk.org where you can post your likes, dislikes and suggestions. I notified the designers to pay attention to this thread. Here is the link...
> http://www.peercointalk.org/index.php?topic=285.0"

A copy of the 99Design Contest Specification is in the Appendix. Sunny King said:

> "Let's be constructive and respect other community members' effort. I certainly appreciate Sentinelrv and other donators contributing time and resource to get a better logo designed. Everyone has their own strength, so let's be positive and concentrate on what one can do to help the
> community grow, rather than discouraging other people's work. Yes talking to others about ppcoin innovation helps too, so you are also doing the good work to help, even if they remain skeptical, it still differentiates our network from all the copycat altcoins out there and will help us gain critical mass at some point."

Sentinelrv also posted another update the following day:

> "Ok guys, a couple of updates.
> - I guaranteed the prize money to double the amount of entries.
> - I just spent another $99 to get 99designs to send out a promotion tweet about our contest to their almost 80,000 designers/followers. I am
>
> completely tapped out now.
> - I just realized that everyone can comment on the contest page and talk to the designers, but you'll most likely have to register an account first.
> - I asked if it was possible to get a time extension since I'm paying for promotion, not sure on this one though."

The last major event of the June concerned the launch of the second crypto by Sunny King. Primecoin was announced on Bitcointalk on the pre-release forum thread titled " [XPM] [ANN] Primecoin Prerelease Announcement - Introducing Prime Proof-of-Work" on the 28th of June at 23:07:15 UTC ready for launch on the 7th of July at about 18:00 UTC. In his weekly update (#45), Sunny King said:

> "I am happy to launch another innovative cryptocurrency design soon. Primecoin project was under development since March. It was meant to complement ppcoin in our technology portfolio. Primecoin introduces the first non-hashcash proof-of-work, prime number proof-of-work, the first proof-of-work in cryptocurrency that not only provides minting and ~security, but also provides additional potential scientific values. This advancement will pave the way for future proof-of-work types with diverse scientific computing values and uses."

Other events which occurred in the month of June were:

- A few extra product or service websites had recently adopted Peercoin as a means of payment alongside already implemented cryptocurrencies. Some of these included "fendlestick's coingas" and "Petr1fied's cryptoblackjack". Sunny King expected further sites to follow on from these in the future as more realise the current and future benefits of utilising cryptocurrency.

- Two more coins forked from the sourcecode of Peercoin had been launched:

> Bottlecaps launched on the 23rd of June at 22:09:56 UTC.
> Crypto Bullion launched on the 27th of June at 17:46:02 UTC (pre-mined).

- A few websites published articles about cryptocurrency in which Peercoin got mentioned or commented on. These were:

> "All About Bitcoin Mining: Road To Riches Or Fool's Gold?"
> (http://www.tomshardware.com/reviews/bitcoin-mining-make-money,3514-9.html)
>
> "Alternative Currencies: Is There Staying Power?"
> (http://www.researchandmarkets.com/research/s5f5c3/alternative)

NEW PEERCOIN LOGO

JULY 2013

I.   Qualifying Round of Peercoin Logo Design Contest ended.

II.   Second Sunny King cryptocurrency called Primecoin launched.

III.   Final Round of Peercoin Logo Design Contest began.

IV.   Logo Design Contest ended with #199 the winner.

V.   Crypto Trade Exchange added the direct XPM/PPC and XPM/USD pairs.

July began with the Peercoin logo design contest on 99Designs being the predominant topic of discussion and participation. Enough money had been raised by the community in order for the silver package on the site to be used. A total of $499 had been raised. At the end of the contest, a total of forty designers had put forward a grand total of two hundred and seventeen potential coin logo designs.

On the 4th of July, the qualifying round for voting for the new coin logo was over. Members of the community had to next vote for their favourite six designers and the submission numbers of their favourite designs on Bitcointalk. Once people had voted for their favourite six designers, the community could then move to the final round. Voting on Bitcointalk was restricted to users who had been signed up to the forum for at least one week and had posted a minimum of twenty posts. The plan was to allow voting to last for about three days depending upon participation.

On the 6th of July, the votes were counted at around 2:00 PM EST by Sentinelrv:

Designer Votes:	Design Votes:	Design Votes:
15 - Lightning	7 - #109	1 - #110
9 - lesdeane	5 - #96	1 - #91
7 - Gamekyuubi	4 - #35	1 - #82
6 - maxwell	3 - #48	1 - #78
4 - PhatCowDesigns	2 - #178	1 - #72
4 - Anamulmasum	2 - #175	1 - #71
4 - Akaki	2 - #156	1 - #67
3 - Miroslav22	2 - #135	1 - #60
3 - art_zone	2 - #124	1 - #58
2 - Degotz Brugack	2 - #80	1 - #49
2 - sco99	2 - #21	1 - #47
2 - Wolf-rainer	2 - #8	1 - #45
2 - hipopo41	1 - #168	1 - #44
2 - 4d33	1 - #167	1 - #33
1 - Masterlogos	1 - #162	1 - #32
1 - Trimiew	1 - #155	1 - #31
1 - mrkar	1 - #148	1 - #7
1 - TBD	1 - #147	
1 - iconsymbolic	1 - #141	
1 - DesignOSS	1 - #121	
1 - Mind1		

As shown above, three designers were tied on four votes each for fifth and sixth position. Sentinelrv said:

> "Here is what we're going to do. You'll all have a second chance to vote here. Out of the three names listed above, you can only vote for two of them, since I only have two more slots to fill. I will give you guys until sometime tonight to vote. If there are no more votes, I'll decide it myself. Post your two votes in the same voting thread at Bitcointalk."

Below are some of the most popular coin logos in the qualifying round. Coin logo design #96 by LesDeaneGraphics was withdrawn, but his #197 is shown below:

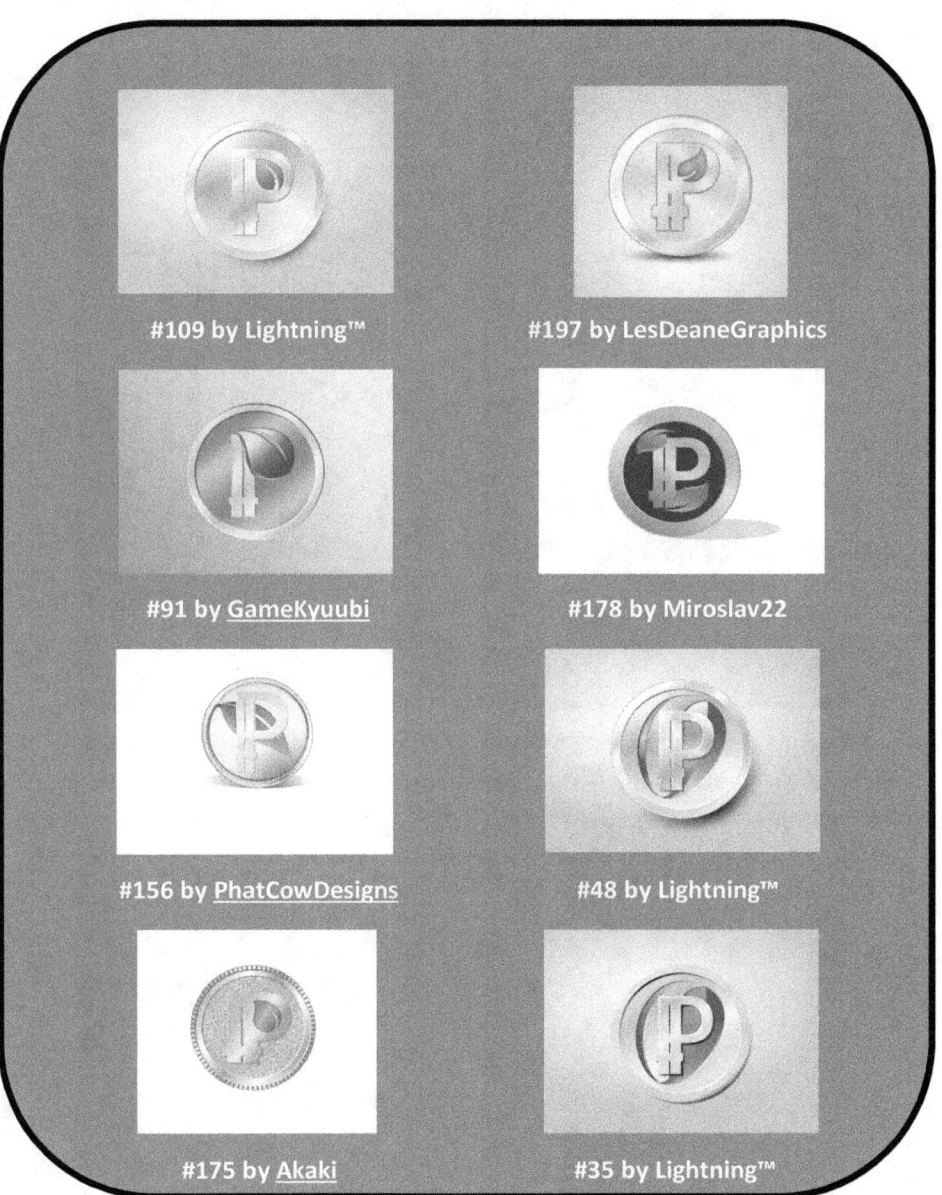

#109 by Lightning™

#197 by LesDeaneGraphics

#91 by GameKyuubi

#178 by Miroslav22

#156 by PhatCowDesigns

#48 by Lightning™

#175 by Akaki

#35 by Lightning™

On the 7th of July at 16:42:39 UTC, Sentinelrv said first round voting had ended:

"1st round voting has now been completed. The clear favorite among most people is the designer Lightning with #109, followed by lesdeane with #96 and Gamekyuubi...

1st Round Designer Votes:	1st Round Design Votes:
15 - Lightning	7 - #109
9 - lesdeane	5 - #96
7 - Gamekyuubi	4 - #35
6 - maxwell	3 - #48
4 - PhatCowDesigns	
4 - Akaki	

We have now entered the final round, which will last three days. The six selected designers can now submit new or updated designs. We need to help them make their revisions. After these three days are up though, there will be no more design time, so this is it. We need to use this time wisely. If you have suggestions, please post them now either on the main contest page or on the new feedback thread at ppcointalk...

http://www.ppcointalk.org/index.php?topic=315.0"

On the same day, Sunny King's newly created cryptocurrency called Primecoin launched. He created a Bitcointalk thread just before the launch at 17:46:50 UTC titled "[XPM] [ANN] Primecoin Release - First Scientific Computing Cryptocurrency".

PRIMECOIN SPECIFICATION SUMMARY

Date of Genesis Block:	5th of July 2013 at 22:47:09 UTC
Date of Launch:	7th of July 2013 at 18:28:00 UTC
Symbol:	XPM, Ψ
Founder:	Sunny King
Hashing Algorithm:	Cunningham (non-hashcash)
Timestamping Alogorithm:	Proof of Work

Sunny King said the Primecoin Project had been under development since March 2013. It was introduced as a means to complement Peercoin to enhance the future of cryptocurrency. Primecoin was the first cryptocurrency to adopt a new form of hashing involving prime number proof of work. It would also help the scientific community in the discovery of chains of prime numbers. In his #46 weekly update on the 8th of July, Sunny King said:

"Primecoin is released! I am happy to announce the second innovative cryptocurrency design has now joined ppcoin as our advanced technology portfolio in the highly competitive cryptocurrency market. Primecoin design and development took a better part of 4 months since March, I am relieved that it is now released to public. I hope this work would further advance cryptocurrency field and inspire other scientific computing proof-of-work types to emerge."

Also on the 8th of July, FuzzyBear posted in the official Peercointalk forum that he had removed some spam accounts from the forum. In doing so, he found that there were a total of 2,850 activated users registered at the time. He also attached a Peercoin block explorer to the forum, but it does not function anymore (http://blockexplorer.ppcointalk.org). However, a new one now exists.

Three days later, Sentinelrv said:

"The final round of voting has begun for the Peercoin logo design contest. Please place your final vote at the link below...

https://bitcointalk.org/index.php?topic=254091.0"

Now the community had the chance to vote for their favourite coin logo designed by one of the prior top six designers. These were Lightning, lesdeane, Gamekyuubi, Maxwell, PhatCowDesigns and Akaki. Voters were asked two questions which were:

1) What is the entry # for your favorite design?

2) What is the reason you chose to vote for this design?

After two days of voting, there was an outright winner. Coin logo #199 by Lightning had been chosen as a representative symbol of Peercoin. Sentinelrv announced the winner on the 13th of July at 05:19:27 UTC on Bitcointalk:

> "Voting is over. #199 wins the contest. Say hello to ppc's new logo!
> Now on to rebuilding the website!"

FuzzyBear praised Sentinelrv and the community for organising and implementing the design contest. He said:

> "Many thanks to Sentinelrv for again all your hard work in keeping this vote / contest running.... would not have happened without you so the community owes you... except for the developers who will now have to make all new builds and website icons and logos!! but seriously thank you from everyone over at http://www.ppcointalk.org/ as well"

On the 28th of July, Sunny King announced on Peercointalk that Crypto Trade had added the direct trading pairs XPM/PPC and XPM/USD. He said:

> "FYI, crypto-trade.com now supports direct
> XPM/PPC and XPM/USD trading:
>
> https://crypto-trade.com/trade/xpm_ppc
> https://crypto-trade.com/trade/xpm_usd
>
> crypto-trade now supports 3 trading pairs for XPM and 2 trading pairs for PPC, including direct USD trading for XPM. Thanks neotrix and team for the excellent support!"

In his weekly update (#49), Sunny King said he would resume the development of a future release build client (v0.4) in the next week or so. These weekly updates now included announcements regarding the progress of Primecoin as well as Peercoin.

By the end of the month, Peercoin was active on six cryptocurrency exchanges (Vircurex, BTC-e, Bter, Cryptsy, Crypto Trade and Coins-e). The following table displays the historical values of Peercoin on the 1st of July and the 31st of July 2013 according to http://www.cryptocoincharts.info/:

	1st of July 2013			31st of July 2013		
	Open (BTC)	High (BTC)	Close (BTC)	Open (BTC)	High (BTC)	Close (BTC)
Vircurex	0.00125001	0.00145000	0.00140001	0.00138011	0.00141988	0.00141988
BTC-e	0.00123000	0.00143000	0.00143000	0.00143000	0.00143000	0.00139000
Bter	0.00123000	0.00139000	0.00136000	0.00109000	0.00109000	0.00109000
Cryptsy	0.00122201	0.00146765	0.00146764	0.00140000	0.00143999	0.00132001
Crypto Trade	0.00130000	0.00130010	0.00120000	0.00135000	0.00135000	0.00135000
Coins-e	NO DATA					

PEERCOIN ONE YEAR ANNIVERSARY

AUGUST 2013

I.   Chat box implemented on the main page of the official forum.

II.   75% of blocks now generated via proof of stake.

III.   Vitalik Buterin of Bitcoin Magazine Interviewed Sunny King.

IV.   Peercoin celebrated its one year anniversary since launch.

V.   Peercoin values on the 19th of August were...

In the last month of the first year of Peercoin, only nineteen days remained until the first anniversary since launch. Only a few events occurred in this period. Discussion on Bitcointalk had become very small as only four comments were made on there from the 1st to the 19th of August. It was now clear that discussion had effectively switched from Bitcointalk to other places such as Peercointalk.

On the 4th of August, FuzzyBear announced on Peercointalk that a "chat box/shout box/troll box" had been created on the main page of the official Peercoin forum. It was implemented as a means for signed up forum users to discuss issues in realtime. For instance, if users require help to find certain Peercoin related material on the forum or just to ask a quick question. Before using it, users must have at least two posts in the forum. The first post in the chat box was made by FuzzyBear who said "testing" at about 9am UTC on the 4th August.

A full chat box history is accessible from which many discussions can be found. It still exists today and is called "PEERCOIN AND PRIMECOIN CHAT".

On the 8th of August, an interview between Sunny King and Vitalik Buterin was held on the Peercointalk chat box. A full transcript of this can be found in the appendix on this book.

On the 17th of August, a user on Peercointalk announced that the number of blocks generated via proof of stake to proof of work had reached a ratio of about 3:1. User "redlee" said:

> "According to theseven's network statistics :
> http://theseven.bounceme.net/~theseven/pool/netstats
>
> Estimated across the last 520 blocks / 59.1 hours:
> System Current hashrate Number of blocks 51% attack hashrate
> Proof of work 2565.2 GH/s 129 (24.8%) 5170.3 GH/s
> Proof of stake 364.3 MH/s 391 (75.2%) 242.2 MH/s
> That was the statistics about 10 hrs ago.
> So 75% blocks are generated out of POS.
> Thoughts?
> And I got another question: currently 308 ppc per block at 1 million difficulty. at what difficulty can we see 2 digit PPC/block?"

On the 19th of August 2013, the Peercoin network protocol was one year old. The last block generated before this occurred was block number 64,852 at 17:50:01 UTC . This was a proof of stake block with a mintage of 0.57 PPC. Proceeding this one, the next block was also proof of stake at 18:22:30 UTC with 0.14 generated.

According to www.cryptocoincharts.info, the average BTC values on Vircurex, BTC-e, Bter, Cryptsy and Crypto Trade were 0.001442395, 0.00144, 0.00146, 0.001425075 and 0.001430055 respectively. There was no data for Coin-e.

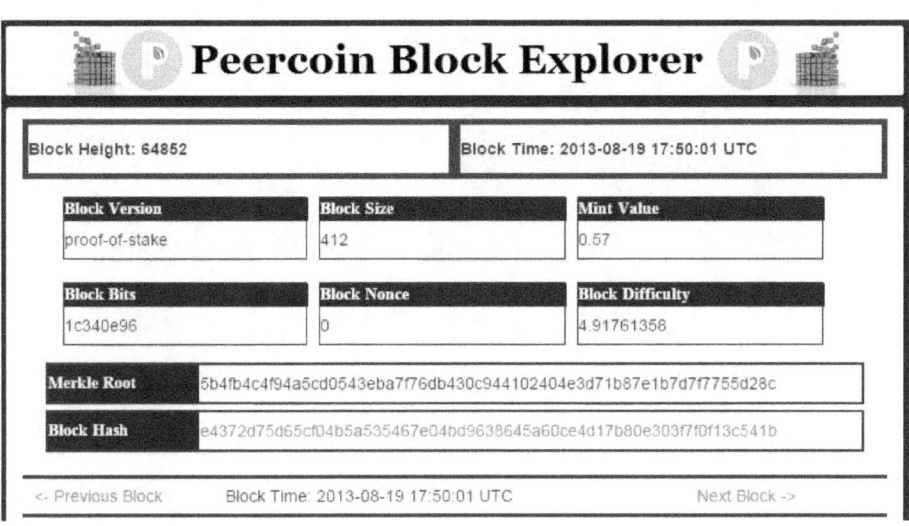

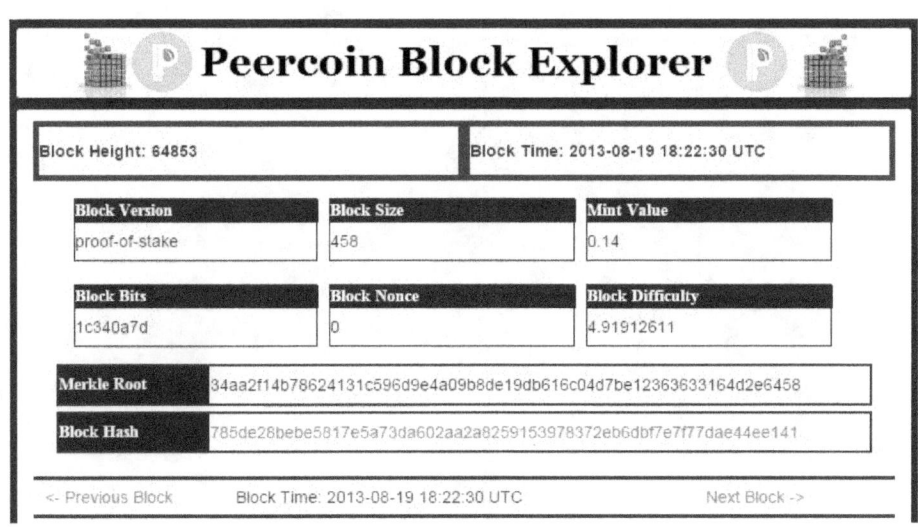

APPENDIX

Contest title (99Designs)

Title— Logo Needed for Peercoin, a Revolutionary Cryptocurrency Designed to Rival Bitcoin!

Subtitle— The world's first energy efficient, environmentally friendly cryptocurrency!

Background information

Description of the organization and its target audience

The logo to be designed is for a cryptocurrency called Peercoin, also known as ppcoin, ppc and Peer to Peer Coin. Cryptocurrencies are a form of digital currency that provide people with the ability to send coins to anyone anywhere in the world at any time without having to worry about large transaction fees. Unlike dollars or paper money, cryptocurrencies cannot be printed out of thin air. This revolutionary feature helps to prevent inflation and devaluation of the currency, helping to maintain its value. Cryptocurrencies also provide anonymity in transactions, take banking out of the equation, as well as many other benefits.

Bitcoin is currently the most popular cryptocurrency, although we plan to change that over time. The problem with Bitcoin is that the security of its network is maintained through a process called mining using a proof of work system where many computers work together to protect the network through computation. There are literally rooms full of electronic equipment dedicated to mining Bitcoin. This leads to a problem where a massive amount of energy is being expended in order to guarantee the security of the network. This problem can only get worse as it becomes more accepted as a mainstream currency, making Bitcoin fundamentally unsustainable in the long-term.

Peercoin attempts to solve this energy problem by combining the proof of work system with proof of stake, which provides the security of the network through a different process and reduces energy expenditure significantly, also allowing for interest to be generated on your accumulated coins. Peercoin is therefore the world's first energy efficient environmentally friendly cryptocurrency.

Industry

Accounting & Financial

Interview between Sunny King and Vitalik Buterin on the 8th of August 2013

Sunny King [08:20 pm]:Nice to see you Vitalik!

Sunny King [08:22 pm]:I am still amazed by your quality technical articles on Bitcoin Magazine

Vitalik Buterin [08:22 pm]:well thank you!

Vitalik Buterin [08:22 pm]:always glad to get feedback so I know what to write more of

Sunny King [08:22 pm]:and to absorb all the materials on primecoin within one day and wrote such nice long article

FuzzyBear [08:23 pm]:yup avid reader here and love your articles as well

Sunny King [08:23 pm]:that's an amazing feat

Vitalik Buterin [08:25 pm]:not many people toe that middle ground line between writing and advanced comp-sci I suppose

Vitalik Buterin [08:25 pm]:Bitcoin (and coins in general) are like that though; brings lots of things together

Vitalik Buterin [08:26 pm]:anyway, I'm a big fan of what you guys are doing here too

Vitalik Buterin [08:26 pm]:I think you're probably the single most original altcoin developer out there

Vitalik Buterin [08:27 pm]:well, there's Ripple too, but in bitcoin terms they're a large corporation

FuzzyBear [08:27 pm]:yup sunny has my vote by a mile

Sunny King [08:27 pm]:Thanks really appreciate it

Vitalik Buterin [08:28 pm]:so, question 1

Vitalik Buterin [08:28 pm]:Who are you? What's your background? Are you Sunny King in real life, or is that just an internet identity?

Sunny King [08:29 pm]:Yeah it's a pen identity, similar to Satoshi's tradition I guess

Vitalik Buterin [08:30 pm]:any hints as to what you do outside of altcoins?

twobits [08:30 pm]:Ripple is not really a coin.

Vitalik Buterin [08:31 pm]:> twobits [08:30 pm]: Ripple is not really a coin. <- I throw it in there because I think it's idea of "consensus" is a serious competitor to PoW/PoS, and brilliant if it can be made to work. It has problems though, no doubt about that

Sunny King [08:32 pm]:Although I didn't really take that extreme measures so at least some of my friends know I am doing this

Sunny King [08:33 pm]:The main reason is that I hope if political climate turns worse in the next couple years that I could still buy some time to make a bit more contributions

Vitalik Buterin [08:34 pm]:do you think it will?

Sunny King [08:34 pm]:I did some c programming before and currently work mostly on cryptocurrency

Sunny King [08:35 pm]:possibly since the events this year already confirmed my concerns (and satoshi's)

Sunny King [08:37 pm]:but I think primecoin could also help to bring another positive argument for cryptocurrency

Vitalik Buterin [08:38 pm]:yep, I agree

Vitalik Buterin [08:40 pm]:I'm staying in Spain right now, and it's interesting how the culture here is much more egalitarian/social oriented than, say, the US would tolerate. Among those who don't like Bitcoin, the two major arguments are (1) early adopter unfairness and (2) mining is wasteful

Vitalik Buterin [08:40 pm]:you've done quite well in solving (2)

Vitalik Buterin [08:41 pm]:do you have any opinion on the early adopter issue?

Sunny King [08:41 pm]:if so I think the market is now trying to wrestle with (1) with all these altcoins

Vitalik Buterin [08:42 pm]:how so?

Sunny King [08:42 pm]:from my point of view I don't think early adopter is an 'issue' per se with bitcoin

Sunny King [08:42 pm]:just like the gold miners and 'hoarders' are not an issue with gold

Sunny King [08:43 pm]:although it does appear to me that the market force behind cryptocurrency is different from precious metals

Sunny King [08:44 pm]:in the old commodity money gold eventually does dominate

Sunny King [08:45 pm]:but it seems much harder for bitcoin to sustain such dominance in cryptocurrency

Vitalik Buterin [08:45 pm]:why do you say that?

Sunny King [08:47 pm]:one observation is that lots of miners and investors are looking at new altcoins hoping to strike it right, even if it is a pure clone without anything new

Vitalik Buterin [08:47 pm]:yeah, I'm finding the interest in pure clones very strange

Sunny King [08:47 pm]:i guess this has to do with the early adopter issue that you mentioned

Vitalik Buterin [08:47 pm]:why do you think people care about them?

Sunny King [08:49 pm]:That also perplexs me a bit but I think the market is treating the currencies as competing companies, you know like stocks

Sunny King [08:50 pm]:But I also found some other deeper elements at work that may undermine bitcoin's dominance eventually

Sunny King [08:51 pm]:this has something to do with bitcoin's scarcity and the specialization of mining hardware

Sunny King [08:52 pm]:which I think underscores the rise of litecoin since last year

Sunny King [08:53 pm]:this I have described a bit in my design paper of primecoin,

Sunny King [08:54 pm]:basically I think bitcoin's overall security against 51% attack would drop in the future against other competing currencies

Vitalik Buterin [08:55 pm]:because the block reward would keep going down

Vitalik Buterin [08:55 pm]:right

Sunny King [08:55 pm]:this could become a basis for it to lose dominance in the long term

Sunny King [08:57 pm]:although this is still speculation and the process likely is still years away

Vitalik Buterin [08:58 pm]:question: isn't primecoin theoretically subject to the same effects?

Vitalik Buterin [08:58 pm]:it's block reward will likely decrease quadratically (assuming Moore's law) and not exponentially, so it will be slower

Sunny King [08:59 pm]:but as a designer I need to be aware of the possibilities so this is part of the reasons for introducing primecoin

Vitalik Buterin [08:59 pm]:but a hundred years down the line they'll both be very low

Sunny King [09:00 pm]:I think designing for a hundred year is unrealistic, but I do look at 20 years and possibly beyond

Sunny King [09:01 pm]:so primecoin tries to weaken the scacity model a bit to compensate for a sustained mining market and higher security

Sunny King [09:02 pm]:bitcoin has a stronger scarcity model than gold, but i think having something closer to gold is good enough

Sunny King [09:03 pm]:so both ppcoin and primecoin take this approach with their scarcity

Vitalik Buterin [09:03 pm]:the inverse quadratic rule, right

Sunny King [09:04 pm]:yeah for primecoin block value is $999/difficulty^2$

Vitalik Buterin [09:05 pm]:question: why not just $999/block number^2$?

Sunny King [09:05 pm]:so when moore's law hit the wall it would become constant generation but still low inflation

Vitalik Buterin [09:05 pm]:with some fudge factor near the beginning

Sunny King [09:06 pm]:this is because I don't like to guess a fixed schedule

Sunny King [09:06 pm]:so I'd rather for market to decide when it should become more scarce

Sunny King [09:08 pm]:so it's design as more miners and better hardware/algorithm would mean lower production

Sunny King [09:08 pm]:the timing is then determined by market

Vitalik Buterin [09:09 pm]:well, it's determined by the market in the exact opposite way that, say, gold supply is determined by the market

Vitalik Buterin [09:09 pm]:gold: more miners/better algorithm -> more supply

Vitalik Buterin [09:09 pm]:is there any conscious reason behind doing it that way?

Sunny King [09:09 pm]:not exactly, it actually still resembles gold

Vitalik Buterin [09:10 pm]:primecoin: more miners/better algorithm -> less supply

Sunny King [09:10 pm]:more supply is temporary, just like say the 2nd week of primecoin there are a lot more production than normal

Vitalik Buterin [09:11 pm]:well, that was the lag in difficulty adjustment

Vitalik Buterin [09:11 pm]:which is a different issue

Sunny King [09:11 pm]:but for gold mining it just appears on a longer time scale so it's less obvious

Vitalik Buterin [09:11 pm]:now, though, my estimate of the final supply of xpm got adjusted down by 50-100 mil after that big spike

Sunny King [09:14 pm]:it's not really different they are connected, for gold mining you are just moving future production to now, it's just over many years so not obvious

Vitalik Buterin [09:15 pm]:hmm, that's an interesting argument actually

Sunny King [09:15 pm]:whereas bitcoin/primecoin adjust difficulty in a week or two

Vitalik Buterin [09:17 pm]:I personally have always wanted a coin with deliberately slow difficulty adjustment (eg. timespan of 3-12 months); seems like that would also approximate gold in a different way

Sunny King [09:18 pm]:that wouldn't work well because block spacing would be destroyed

Vitalik Buterin [09:18 pm]:true

Sunny King [09:19 pm]:for example several altcoins got stuck at high difficulty after the first few days

Vitalik Buterin [09:19 pm]:maybe make difficulty adjustment rapid but increase the reward for some time instead...

Vitalik Buterin [09:19 pm]:thrree are many ideas

Sunny King [09:19 pm]:it's generally agreed now that bitcoin's 2-week adjustment schedule is not suitable for a new altcoin

Vitalik Buterin [09:20 pm]:the problem there wasn't the 2-week schedule, so much as the 2016 block schedule

Vitalik Buterin [09:20 pm]:if your diff is 10x too high, that

Vitalik Buterin [09:20 pm]:is 20 weeks

Vitalik Buterin [09:21 pm]:anyway, I saw you made an interesting post a month ago on the ppcointalk forums

Vitalik Buterin [09:21 pm]:http://www.ppcointalk.org/index....sg1715

Sunny King [09:21 pm]:yeah this problem was actually hit by namecoin, the first altcoin so they developed merge mining for this

Sunny King [09:22 pm]:yeah that's strategic reason for the design of primecoin

Vitalik Buterin [09:22 pm]:talking about what your strategy with Primecoin was

Vitalik Buterin [09:24 pm]:so you think that the proof-of-* mechanism is essentially the major part of Bitcoin that can be improved, and want the community to focus more on looking for and promoting solid alternatives

Sunny King [09:24 pm]:of course first I had to have the idea that a primecoin could technically work, but then i am looking for reasons why we should run two coins so primecoin can be made

Vitalik Buterin [09:24 pm]:is that accurate?

Sunny King [09:25 pm]:so that's primecoin strategic reason

Sunny King [09:26 pm]:So from late last year litecoin has spectacular rise that made me think about why and the competive position of ppcoin vs litecoin

Sunny King [09:27 pm]:it's possible that market would favor something simpler than ppcoin in the shorter term e.g. next couple years

Sunny King [09:28 pm]:so primecoin would be a good candidate in the sense that it's designed to have most litecoin's so-called advantage over bitcoin

Sunny King [09:29 pm]:yet still being innovative and brings new ideas

Vitalik Buterin [09:30 pm]:in terms of new ideas

Vitalik Buterin [09:31 pm]:I saw somewhere, whether in the source code or the discussions, that you were working on some kind of improved checkpointing system for ppcoin and/or primecoin

Vitalik Buterin [09:31 pm]:something not quite so centralized

Sunny King [09:32 pm]:yeah its already in primecoin, it's an updated version of ppcoin's checkpoint system

Sunny King [09:33 pm]:even ppcoin's checkpoint is not meant to stay centralized forever

Sunny King [09:33 pm]:and it's going to work similarly in ppcoin in the future as well

Vitalik Buterin [09:34 pm]:so how does this new checkpointing system work?

Sunny King [09:36 pm]:basically developers can broadcast a checkpoint to the network, and if an user turns on the checkpoint enforcement in the node then it would follow the block chain fork of the checkpoint

Sunny King [09:37 pm]:this means that if the majority of network enforces the checkpoints then developer has power to thwart a sustained 51% attack

Sunny King [08|Aug 09:38 pm]:while the network is turning into a temporary centralization mode

Sunny King [09:38 pm]:although there are built-in checks to ensure even in the checkpoint mode developers cannot arbitrarily abuse his power

Vitalik Buterin [09:38 pm]:how did the system work before?

Sunny King [09:39 pm]:in ppcoin right now the checkpoints are enforced by default so users have no say in whether to follow it or not

Vitalik Buterin [09:40 pm]:ah, okay, so hardcoded into software essentially

Sunny King [09:40 pm]:yeah but it will be switched over in the future

Vitalik Buterin [09:41 pm]:> although there are built-in checks to ensure even in the checkpoint mode developers cannot arbitrarily abuse his power <- what kinds of built-in checks are you talking about?

Sunny King [09:41 pm]:the system is designed because threat of 51% attack is real with altcoins

Sunny King [09:42 pm]:there is a consistency check with checkpoints,

Sunny King [09:43 pm]:meaning that developers cannot issue conflicting checkpoints and force double-spending on the network

Sunny King [09:44 pm]:for example, say developer checkpoint is issued on a block with 6-confirmations, then you can treat the transaction confirmed earlier than the checkpoint is safe

Sunny King [09:45 pm]:he cannot invalidate that checkpoint and ask the network to go into another block chain fork

Vitalik Buterin [09:45 pm]:what if a developer sends two conflicting checkpoints to two parts of the network at the same time?

Vitalik Buterin [09:46 pm]:so half picks up one first, half picks up the other

Sunny King [09:47 pm]:that would cause the network to fork and requires manual intervention like restarting or upgrading client

Vitalik Buterin [09:48 pm]:okay, makes sense

Vitalik Buterin [09:48 pm]:if it was perfect, you would just use it instead of the pow/pos in the first place

Sunny King [09:48 pm]:in primecoin user could also then ignore checkpoint and just follow the fork with more work

Sunny King [09:50 pm]:checkpoint is a temporary centralization defense against 51%, not on the same level as PoW or PoS

Vitalik Buterin [09:50 pm]:is it a jsonrpc command to do this, or are you planning on adding a GUI as well?

Sunny King [09:51 pm]:oh the Qt now has debug window which can do all the rpc commands

Vitalik Buterin [09:51 pm]:right, forgot about that

Vitalik Buterin [09:52 pm]:so what are the next steps / near-term goals in primecoin development at this point?

Sunny King [09:52 pm]:but if needed we could add it as an option setting

Sunny King [09:54 pm]:I think infrastructure and marketing would be the top priority for primecoin, more exchange support, mining pools and so on

Sunny King [09:55 pm]:the team is also expanded quite a bit so primecoin shouldn't lag behind while I work on ppcoin v0.4

Vitalik Buterin [09:57 pm]:are you planning on integrating the latest btc features eventually? (eg. payment protocol)

Sunny King [09:58 pm]:sure both primecoin and ppcoin should keep reasonably up-to-date with bitcoin features

Sunny King [09:58 pm]:right now primecoin is ahead of ppcoin in this regard

Vitalik Buterin [10:00 pm]:what is ppcoin 0.4 going to have? The advanced check-pointing system?

Sunny King [10:02 pm]:It's mainly a refresh to bitcoin v0.8 features, but there could also be some adjustment on certain protocols

Sunny King [10:04 pm]:the checkpoint would be adjusted a bit also but it won't be as decentralized as in primecoin yet

Sunny King [10:05 pm]:btw ppcoin now has numerous copies in the market and i have now stopped counting them

Vitalik Buterin [08|Aug 10:06 pm]:yeah it seems like proof of stake is slowly becoming more accepted

Vitalik Buterin [08|Aug 10:06 pm]:also, as far as proofs go, in the ppcoin paper you mentioned a third possibility

Sunny King [10:06 pm]:just past several weeks saw at least three copies released in china and went into speculative frenzy

Vitalik Buterin [10:06 pm]:"proof of excellence"

Vitalik Buterin [10:06 pm]:could you elaborate a bit more on that idea?

Sunny King [10:08 pm]:it's a concept although there is no concrete designs around this concept

Sunny King [10:09 pm]:it's based on that a tournament result of some games is difficult to forge

Sunny King [10:09 pm]:for example you cannot go to a tennis tournament to win prizes without having some serious skills

Vitalik Buterin [10:10 pm]:so a coin might have some kind of internal AI tournament?

Vitalik Buterin [10:10 pm]:best programmers win and get to mine some blocks

Sunny King [10:10 pm]:so it's a possible candidate to replace the functions of proof-of-work

Sunny King [10:11 pm]:Yeah that's the idea

Sunny King [10:12 pm]:It doesn't have to be AI it can be done between humans as well

Vitalik Buterin [10:13 pm]:true

Vitalik Buterin [10:13 pm]:although coins don't really have a way of distinguishing between human players and bots

Vitalik Buterin [10:14 pm]:the only challenge I know of that humans are better at is Go

Sunny King [10:14 pm]:right and most games AI can play better than human

Sunny King [10:15 pm]:I actually looked at Go and I think even for that the network would be dominated by bots

Sunny King [10:15 pm]:because there is already very good Go AI and very few pro level Go players

Vitalik Buterin [10:15 pm]:yeah

Vitalik Buterin [10:16 pm]:and ideally you do want the system to be somewhat egalitarian

Vitalik Buterin [10:16 pm]:as otherwise one party might get 51%

Vitalik Buterin [10:16 pm]:eg. whoever has the best go algorithm

Vitalik Buterin [10:17 pm]:that's probably the hard part about implementingit

Sunny King [10:17 pm]:that's one of its issues because its distribution is a lot more concentrated than proof-of-work

Sunny King [10:20 pm]:Vitalik do you sense a general change of attitude toward altcoins?

Vitalik Buterin [10:21 pm]:yes

Vitalik Buterin [10:21 pm]:I can feel it

Sunny King [10:21 pm]:I am actually quite surprised that Bitcoin Magazine carried primecoin the first day since my impression earlier was that there was no interest

Vitalik Buterin [10:21 pm]:six months ago, altcoins were almost irrelevant

Sunny King [10:22 pm]:and only time i saw anything mentioned was ripple

Vitalik Buterin [10:22 pm]:consider this

Vitalik Buterin [10:22 pm]:teleport yourself to Dec 2008

Vitalik Buterin [10:22 pm]:simultaneously release bitcoin and primecoin

Vitalik Buterin [10:22 pm]:which one do you think people will like more?

Vitalik Buterin [10:23 pm]:I think primecoin might be the first one to actually beat Bitcoin on that test

Vitalik Buterin [10:23 pm]:litecoin was nice, but scrypt is overcomplicated

Vitalik Buterin [10:23 pm]:ppcoin is, as you said, too complex

Vitalik Buterin [10:24 pm]:Ripple is also too complex

Vitalik Buterin [10:25 pm]:it can only survive because Bitcoin came first to ease people into the idea of cryptocurrency

Vitalik Buterin [10:26 pm]:I think people are slowly realizing that there are still serious improvements to the core idea of cryptocurrency that can be made

Vitalik Buterin [10:26 pm]:and at the same time the community got big enough to support them all

Vitalik Buterin [10:28 pm]:here in Calafou (place in Spain), ever since I introduced the locals to Primecoin people have been thinking, since we have one example of a useful PoW, what else can we do?

Sunny King [10:29 pm]:yeah i got a few messages regarding ideas of other useful work types

Vitalik Buterin [10:29 pm]:we came up with the idea of an AI challenge-based coin independently too (although no progress toward anything practical)

Vitalik Buterin [10:30 pm]:what do you think are some promising directions?

Sunny King [10:30 pm]:that's what I hope primecoin would inspire other designers to do

Sunny King [10:32 pm]:I am not sure, there seems quite a bit demand to monetize F@H, and I heard Pande is looking at the matter seriously

Sunny King [10:33 pm]:But it's not easy to come up with a proper decentralized design

Sunny King [10:35 pm]:The things is, the innovative systems are quite costly to develop, and the market doesn't seem to reward original ideas that well in the altcoin arena

Vitalik Buterin [10:35 pm]:F@H?

Vitalik Buterin [10:36 pm]:ah, folding at home

Sunny King [10:36 pm]:So i have seen a lot of such attempts fail because of lack of funding for development

Vitalik Buterin [10:36 pm]:yeah, the problem there is how you make it uncheatable

Vitalik Buterin [10:38 pm]:alright, anything else you wanted to talk about?

Sunny King [10:38 pm]:that's a good chat thanks a lot Vitalik

Sunny King [10:39 pm]:yeah we've covered quite a bit

Vitalik Buterin [10:39 pm]:alright, thank you too!

Sunny King [10:40 pm]:Looking forward to chatting with you again in the future

Peercoin Original Design White Paper
August 2012

PPCoin: Peer-to-Peer Crypto-Currency with Proof-of-Stake

Sunny King, Scott Nadal
(*sunnyking9999@gmail.com, scott.nadal@gmail.com*)

August 19th, 2012

Abstract

A peer-to-peer crypto-currency design derived from Satoshi Nakamoto's Bitcoin. Proof-of-stake replaces proof-of-work to provide most of the network security. Under this hybrid design proof-of-work mainly provides initial minting and is largely non-essential in the long run. Security level of the network is not dependent on energy consumption in the long term thus providing an energy-efficient and more cost-competitive peer-to-peer crypto-currency. Proof-of-stake is based on coin age and generated by each node via a hashing scheme bearing similarity to Bitcoin's but over limited search space. Block chain history and transaction settlement are further protected by a centrally broadcasted checkpoint mechanism.

Introduction

Since the creation of Bitcoin (Nakamoto 2008), proof-of-work has been the predominant design of peer-to-peer crypto currency. The concept of proof-of-work has been the backbone of minting and security model of Nakamoto's design.

In October 2011, we have realized that, the concept of *coin age* can facilitate an alternative design known as *proof-of-stake*, to Bitcoin's proof-of-work system. We have since formalized a design where proof-of-stake is used to build the security model of a peer-to-peer crypto currency and part of its minting process, whereas proof-of-work mainly facilitates the initial part of the minting process and gradually reduces its significance. This design attempts to demonstrate the viability of future peer-to-peer crypto-currencies with no dependency on energy consumption. We have named the project *ppcoin*.

Coin Age

The concept of coin age was known to Nakamoto at least as early as 2010 and used in Bitcoin to help prioritize transactions, for example, although it didn't play much of an critical role in Bitcoin's security model. Coin age is simply defined as currency amount times holding period. In a simple to understand example, if Bob received 10 coins from Alice and held it for 90 days, we say that Bob has accumulated 900 coin-days of coin age.

Additionally, when Bob spent the 10 coins he received from Alice, we say the coin age Bob accumulated with these 10 coins had been *consumed* (or *destroyed*).

131

In order to facilitate the computation of coin age, we introduced a timestamp field into each transaction. Block timestamp and transaction timestamp related protocols are strengthened to secure the computation of coin age.

Proof-of-Stake

Proof-of-work helped to give birth to Nakamoto's major breakthrough, however the nature of proof-of-work means that the crypto-currency is dependent on energy consumption, thus introducing significant cost overhead in the operation of such networks, which is borne by the users via a combination of inflation and transaction fees. As the mint rate slows in Bitcoin network, eventually it could put pressure on raising transaction fees to sustain a preferred level of security. One naturally asks whether we must maintain energy consumption in order to have a decentralized crypto-currency? Thus it is an important milestone both theoretically and technologically, to demonstrate that the security of peer-to-peer crypto-currencies does not have to depend on energy consumption.

A concept termed proof-of-stake was discussed among Bitcoin circles as early as 2011. Roughly speaking, proof-of-stake means a form of proof of ownership of the currency. Coin age consumed by a transaction can be considered a form of proof-of-stake. We independently discovered the concept of proof-of-stake and the concept of coin age in October 2011, whereby we realized that proof-of-stake can indeed replace most proof-of-work's functions with careful redesign of Bitcoin's minting and security model. This is mainly because, similar to proof-of-work, proof-of-stake cannot be easily forged. Of course, this is one of the critical requirements of monetary systems - difficulty to counterfeit. Philosophically speaking, money is a form of 'proof-of-work' in the past thus should be able to substitute proof-of-work all by itself.

Block Generation under Proof-of-Stake

In our hybrid design, blocks are separated into two different types, proof-of-work blocks and proof-of-stake blocks.

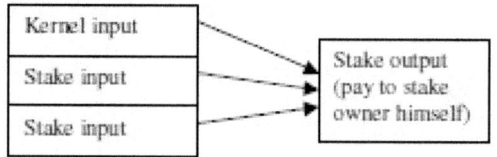

Figure: Structure of Proof-of-Stake (Coinstake) Transaction

The proof-of-stake in the new type of blocks is a special transaction called *coinstake* (named after Bitcoin's special transaction *coinbase*). In the coinstake transaction block owner pays himself thereby consuming his coin age, while gaining the privilege of generating a block for the network and minting for proof-of-stake. The first input of coinstake is called *kernel* and is required to meet certain hash target protocol, thus making the generation of proof-of-stake blocks a stochastic process similar to proof-of-work blocks. However an important difference is that the hashing operation is done over a limited search space (more specifically one hash per unspent wallet-output per second) instead of an unlimited search space as in proof-of-work, thus no significant consumption of energy is involved.

The hash target that stake kernel must meet is a target per unit coin age (coin-day) consumed in the kernel (in contrast to Bitcoin's proof-of-work target which is a fixed target value applying to every node). Thus the more coin age consumed in the kernel, the easier meeting the hash target protocol. For example, if Bob has a wallet-output which accumulated 100 coin-years and expects it to generate a kernel in 2 days, then Alice can roughly expect her 200 coin-year wallet-output to generate a kernel in 1 day.

In our design both proof-of-work hash target and proof-of-stake hash target are adjusted continuously rather than Bitcoin's two-week adjustment interval, to avoid sudden jump in network generation rate.

Minting based on Proof-of-Stake

A new minting process is introduced for proof-of stake blocks in addition to Bitcoin's proof-of-work minting. Proof-of-stake block mints coins based on the consumed coin age in the coinstake transaction. A mint rate of 1 cent per coin-year consumed is chosen to give rise to a low future inflation rate.

Even though we kept proof-of-work as part of the minting process to facilitate initial minting, it is conceivable that in a pure proof-of-stake system initial minting can be seeded completely in genesis block via a process similar to stock market initial public offer (IPO).

Main Chain Protocol

The protocol for determining which competing block chain wins as main chain has been switched over to use consumed coin age. Here every transaction in a block contributes its consumed coin age to the score of the block. The block chain with highest total consumed coin age is chosen as main chain.

This is in contrast to the use of proof-of-work in Bitcoin's main chain protocol, whereas the total work of the block chain is used to determine main chain.

This design alleviates some of the concerns of Bitcoin's 51% assumption, where the system is only considered secure when good nodes control at least 51% of network mining power. First the cost of controlling significant stake might be higher than the cost of acquiring significant mining power, thus raising the cost of attack for such powerful entities. Also attacker's coin age is consumed during the attack, which may render it more difficult for the attacker to continue preventing transactions from entering main chain.

Checkpoint: Protection of History

One of the disadvantages of using total consumed coin age to determine main chain is that it lowers the cost of attack on the entire block chain of history. Even though Bitcoin has relatively strong protection over the history Nakamoto still introduced checkpoints in 2010 as a mechanism to solidify the block chain history, preventing any possible changes to the part of block chain earlier than the checkpoint.

Another concern is that the cost of double-spending attack may have been lowered as well, as attacker may just need to accumulate certain amount of coin age and force reorganization of the block chain. To make commerce practical under such a system, we decided to introduce an additional form of checkpoints that are broadcasted centrally, at much shorter intervals such as a few times daily, to serve to freeze block chain and finalize transactions. This new type of checkpoint is broadcasted similar to Bitcoin's alert system.

Laurie (2011) has argued that Bitcoin has not completely solved the distributed concensus problem as the mechanism for checkpointing is not distributed. We attempted to design a practical distributed checkpointing protocol but found it difficult to secure against network split attack. Although the broadcasted checkpointing mechanism is a form of centralization, we consider it acceptable before a distributed solution is available.

Another technical reason entails the use of centrally broadcasted checkpointing. In order to defend against a type of denial-of-service attack coinstake kernel must be verified before a proof-of-stake block can be accepted into the local database (block tree) of each node. Due to Bitcoin node's data model (transaction index specifically) a deadline of checkpointing is needed to ensure all nodes' capability of verifying connection of each coinstake kernel before accepting a block into the block tree. Because of the above practical considerations we decided not to modify node's data model but use central checkpointing instead. Our solution is to modify the coin age computation to require a minimum age, such as one month, below which the coin age is computed as zero. Then the central checkpointing is used to ensure all nodes can agree upon past transactions older than one month thus allowing the verification of coinstake kernel connection as a kernel requires non-zero coin age thus must use an output from more than one month ago.

Block Signatures and Duplicate Stake Protocol

Each block must be signed by its owner to prevent the same proof-of-stake from being copied and used by attackers.

A duplicate-stake protocol is designed to defend against an attacker using a single proof-of-stake to generate a multitude of blocks as a denial-of-service attack. Each node collects the (kernel, timestamp) pair of all coinstake transactions it has seen. If a received block contains a duplicate pair as another previously received block, we ignore such duplicate-stake block until a successor block is received as an orphan block.

Energy Efficiency

When the proof-of-work mint rate approaches zero, there is less and less incentive to mint proof-of-work blocks. Under this long term scenario energy consumption in the network may drop to very low levels as disinterested miners stop mining proof-of-work blocks. The Bitcoin network faces such risk unless transaction volume/fee rises to high enough levels to sustain the energy consumption. Under our design even if energy consumption approaches zero the network is still protected by proof-of-stake. We call a crypto-currency *long-term energy-efficient* if energy consumption on proof-of-work is allowed to approach zero.

Other Considerations

We modified the proof-of-work mint rate to be not determined by block height (time) but instead determined by difficulty. When mining difficulty goes up, proof-of-work mint rate is lowered. A relatively smooth curve is chosen as opposed to Bitcoin's step functions, to avoid artificially shocking the market. More specifically, a continuous curve is chosen such that each 16x raise of mining difficulty halves the block mint amount.

Over longer term the proof-of-work mint curve would not be too dissimilar to that of Bitcoin in terms of the inflationary behavior, given the continuation of Moore's Law. We consider it wise to follow the traditional observation that the Market favors a low-inflation currency over a high-inflation one, despite of significant criticism of Bitcoin from some mainstream economists due to ideological reasons in our opinion.

Babaioff et al. (2011) studied the effect of transaction fee and argued that transaction fee is an incentive to not cooperate between miners. Under our system this attack is exacerbated so we no longer give transaction fees to block owner. We decided to destroy transaction fees instead. This removes the incentive to not acknowledge other minter's blocks. It also serves as a deflationary force to counter the inflationary force from the proof-of-stake minting.

We also choose to enforce transaction fees at protocol level to defend against block bloating attack.

During our research we have also discovered a third possibility besides proof-of-work and proof-of-stake, which we termed *proof-of-excellence*. Under this system typically a tournament is held periodically to mint coins based on the performance of the tournament participants, mimicking the prizes of real-life tournaments. Although this system tends to consume energy as well when artificial intelligence excels at the game involved, we still found the concept interesting even under such situation as it provides a somewhat intelligent form of energy consumption.

Conclusion

Upon validation of our design in the Market, we expect proof-of-stake designs to become a potentially more competitive form of peer-to-peer crypto-currency to proof-of-work designs due to the elimination of dependency on energy consumption, thereby achieving lower inflation/lower transaction fees at comparable network security levels.

Acknowledgement

Many thanks to Richard Smith for helping out with testing and various network/fork related work.

We would like to thank Satoshi Nakamoto and Bitcoin developers whose brilliant pioneering work opened our minds and made a project like this possible.

References

Babaioff M. et al. (2011): On Bitcoin and red balloons.

Laurie B. (2011): Decentralised currencies are probably impossible (but let's at least make them efficient). (http://www.links.org/files/decentralised-currencies.pdf)

Nakamoto S. (2008): Bitcoin: A peer-to-peer electronic cash system. (http://www.bitcoin.org/bitcoin.pdf)